Stephen Simon: The Director's Journey

STEPHEN SIMON   STEPHEN SIMON   STEPHEN SIMON

Being given the wonderful honor of writing a chapter on "the director's journey" immediately presented quite an unexpected spiritual challenge. As you will read below and see in the film, vulnerability is a major cornerstone of the film. That being said, I must first address a very important question:

Just who *did* direct CWG?

On one level, I was indeed the one out there every day doing all the things that directors get to do: supervising the script development with my wonderful partners in that aspect, designing the look and feel of the film with my incredible collaborator Joao, casting and rehearsing with the extraordinary actors, working with Sherril (the most talented, dedicated, and patient film editor ever born), listening as Emilio created the most haunting and mystical score I have ever heard, and getting to call "Action" and "Cut" (not to mention the incredible taste of breakfast burritos at 5AM). It also illuminated again for me an essential aspect of filmmaking: that it is a collaborative art form. Films are the result of the magical alchemy of dozens of people, and that's also why I simply do not understand how any director can have the chutzpah to take a "Film by . . ." credit. Creative collaborations are what make the process itself so exciting. All that and much more created an experience for me where I quite simply had more fun that I have ever had in my life. On another and much more important level, however, I was simply the conduit through which this extraordinary experience manifested. Simply put, there was no way in this world, or any world for that matter, that I could have actually directed this film.

So . . . this "journey" must begin with me stating very clearly that *Conversations with God* was directed *through* me, not *by* me. I simply got out of the way and allowed the vision of the film to manifest.

Who did direct it?

As each magical moment occurred, it was always my mantra to myself and to everyone else that *Conversations with God* was the result of "casting by God, weather by Goddess." As to the latter aspect, I'm afraid that the Goddess aspect is under-credited so I need to expand a bit on that.

One of the great and powerful messages of *Conversations with God* and all spirituality is that each one of us encounters and defines the Divine Presence in our lives in very unique and individual ways. In my experience, that presence is the Divine Feminine and it is *that* presence that directed this film through me. (My life is a none-too-subtle reflection of that energy: a sister, two stepsisters, four daughters, a granddaughter, and my beloved 13-year-old female Labrador.) Every morning I would ask that Goddess energy to guide me, help me, and illuminate the pathway ahead. And, every day magic and miracles would confirm for me that I just needed to keep out of my own way—and hers—for the film to become all that we dreamed it would be.

Let's just use "weather" as an example:

- We had every weather pattern in the spectrum just when, where, and for as long as we needed them.

- It rained when we needed it, and was sunny when we wanted that.

- On the exact day we needed a spectacular sunrise at Emigrant Lake we got precisely that. On all the other days we shot there, the weather was cold and foggy in the mornings—also exactly what we needed.

- We had foggy mornings just on the days we needed them, and the fog lingered only so long as it was needed to complete the scenes.

- One day it was foggy just long enough to complete a crucial scene. We wanted wind to clear out the fog so we could shoot the scene where Neale decides to leave the park: the "winds of change," so to speak. Right on cue, the fog cleared away instantly by a huge wind which came exactly when we needed it.

- Even though the local forecast called for an almost one hundred percent chance of torrential rains for the evening when we were shooting The Festival of Light, it barely drizzled until the parade and the once-a-year event was over and we had filmed everything we needed.

- I wanted fog for the dawn shot of the cemetery and we again got exactly that. On the days immediately preceding and following that morning, there was no fog.

- We had written snow into one sequence never really thinking that it would actually happen ("What fools we foolish mortals be.") It snows hard enough in Medford, Oregon to actually be visible on film on maybe four or five days a year. When we needed it, the snow came down in huge flakes just until I said "Cut" on the last take, and then it stopped.

Weather by Goddess, indeed.

Casting?

We were gifted with the most exceptional cast. From Henry (about whom I will have much more to say) who was in every scene, to the actors who were with us for only one scene, we were blessed by amazing talent. Except for Henry (to whom we offered the role without having even met him), everyone else in the cast "just happened" to show up in Ashland, Oregon to audition. Just happened? Sure. Right. As I said before, casting by God.

One personal note about our cast: I love and respect actors more than I can possibly express. To allow oneself to be open and vulnerable on the screen takes a very particular and rare kind of emotional courage. Recognizing that, I feel that it is imperative for a director to create and vigilantly maintain a nurturing atmosphere of love and support for actors on and around the set. Only if an actor is protected, heard, trusted, and appreciated can they do their best work. I believe that the performances in the film all reflect that energy, and it was my honor to be there to witness that essence take form. I have been gratified by the response to the performances in the film and have been a bit embarrassed to receive kind words about my direction of the actors. While I am deeply gratified by those comments, please know that the actors deserve all the credit. What was the "secret"? Hiring wonderful actors, creating a loving and supportive atmosphere where they feel safe, being organized and having a comprehensive vision of the film that you communicate clearly, offering a word of advice from time to time, and staying out of the way!

Another example: we completed the twenty-five day shooting schedule on time and on budget when almost the entire film was shot while Mercury was retrograde!

Realizing all that very early on made the whole film possible. The process and everything about it was just way too magical, way too blessed and way too miraculous for any human being to "do." Sure, I knew what I wanted the film to be . . . to feel like . . . to taste like . . . but knowing where all that guidance originated from was what really allowed me to go out there and work every day.

Okay, with that framework in mind I feel a bit more at ease to discuss the director's journey of *CWG*. (Creatively producing the film presented a whole different set of challenges in that the two functions are sometimes inherently at conflict with each other. The director "me" had many a spirited conversation with the producer "me." Going more deeply into that aspect would take a chapter unto itself . . . and probably lead me right back into extensive therapy . . . so it's probably best to leave it at that.)

My film career has been dominated by the quest to make films out of three extraordinary books: the first two as a producer and the third as director/producer. First, it was *Somewhere in Time,* which took almost five years from the time I first read it until the film was released. Next was *What Dreams May Come,* which took almost twenty years. Now, *Conversations with God,* which has been in my head and, most importantly, my heart, for almost ten years. At various times during those years I wondered and even doubted if any of those films would actually happen. *Somewhere in Time* finally crystallized when my late friend Christopher Reeve agreed to play the lead. *What Dreams May Come* came together when Interscope and Ted Field signed on to arrange the financing. *CWG* came together when The Spiritual Cinema Circle became successful enough to provide the financing to both make a deal with Neale and to take the lead in financing the film.

All three projects presented fascinating creative challenges. In *Somewhere in Time* it was the time travel conundrum. In *What Dreams May Come* it was the after-death journey. With *CWG* the challenge was: "Who's going to be the voice of God? How are you going to make a movie out of that book? What's it going to be—'My Dinner with God'?"

Neale's commentary in the previous chapter beautifully details how, from a writing standpoint, we came to answer the last two questions and choose the story structure of the film. I hope the answer to the first question, as it relates to the final scene of the film, will please and perhaps surprise you. As to Neale himself, most of us can only imagine what it must feel like to see your life portrayed on screen. Neale delved deeply into that vulnerability by allowing and even insisting that we portray some of his darker side. *That* kind of courage is unique beyond words. So, thank you for all that, Neale, and thank you from all of us who shepherded this extraordinary work and your life's journey from book to film. I can only hope that you will always be as proud of the film as all of us are who contributed to it. I love you pal, for being you and for doing your work on the planet.

As a director, my very first, and most passionate, guiding principle was that this film had to be from and of the heart . . . for us as filmmakers and for the audience. On every level, it is and was my intention and heart's desire that this movie be experienced primarily on a level of "feeling," such as:

- The emotion of living through one's darkest nightmare and then transcending into the realm of your heart's desire and your soul's destiny

- The pure joy of consciously being in direct connection to the Divine, however you might define that presence . . . and discovering a whole new level of feeling of what that Divine Presence may mean in our lives (Neale was in that presence while writing the book and I certainly experienced it every moment while directing the film.)

- Coming to feel on a soul level who we are and why we are here

- Feeling better about ourselves as human beings and feeling in our hearts who we can be as a humanity when we operate at our very best

- Experiencing on film the dawning of the Age of the Divine Feminine

- Feeling the vulnerability of a heart cracked wide open.

These are the interlocking themes of the film, and the very foundation of spiritual cinema itself. These themes also elicit deeply personal feelings in all of us as individuals; therefore, illuminating them on a movie screen required that we create as much latitude as possible for individual interpretation. For that reason, there are many aspects of CWG that will be experienced—and understood—very differently by each audience member.

The first musical scene at the lake, the post-lecture scene, and the ending of the film are among the scenes in the film that will be subject, I believe, to many conversations about what they may "mean." As these scenes were the very first images that occurred to me while we were developing the film, I certainly know what they represent to me. I also know that others will glean completely different feelings and interpretations from them. In fact, spirituality is such an individual experience that a film which so explicitly and consciously addresses spiritual matters would have to and should evoke a wide variety of emotional responses. To that I can only say, "Yes, I certainly hope so!"

As to providing my own interpretation of what these scenes mean to me, I am reminded of the questions we received about "where the watch actually began" in *Somewhere in Time*. To this question we would always answer, "Somewhere in time!" Truly, delving any more deeply into the details of the vision we all created together for CWG would, I believe, be self-serving at best and, at worst, a complete disservice to you—the audience who will experience the film on your own terms and within your own emotions.

As I was contemplating how to end this chapter, I saw a sign on a nearby house:
The Goddess is alive . . . and there is magic afoot.
Amen . . . and awomen . . . to that.

Stephen Simon
Ashland, Oregon

Stephen Simon was born into filmmaking. His father, S. Sylvan Simon, produced and directed movies in the 1930s and 1940s, including hits like *Born Yesterday* and comedies with Abbott and Costello. Tragically, his father died suddenly at age 39, but Stephen's movie legacy continued when his mother remarried film producer Armand Deutsch. Adopted by his step-father, Stephen became known as Stephen Deutsch for much of his professional career, including for the production of *Somewhere in Time*. But first, there was a college education and a law degree to be earned, though Stephen practiced law for only a year until the lure of the film business caused him to prevail on family friend and legendary producer Ray Stark (*Funny Girl, The World of Suzie Wong, Night of the Iguana, The Way We Were*) at Columbia Pictures for an entry-level job with no office and $200 a week in February 1976.

Later, as both a producer and a studio executive, Stephen would produce or be responsible as an executive for more than twenty feature films with titles that almost define his generation: *Smokey and the Bandit* (1977), *The Goodbye Girl* (1977), *The Electric Horseman* (1979), *All the Right Moves* (1983), *Bill and Ted's Excellent Adventure* (1989), and a personal collaboration with author Richard Matheson which eventually led to Stephen's most defini-tive productions to date: *Somewhere in Time* (1980) and *What Dreams May Come* (1998). On television, Stephen's movie production credits include *The Linda McCartney Story* (2000) and *Homeless to Harvard: The Liz Murray Story* (2003). Stephen admits that his involvement in *Body of Evidence* (1993) with pop diva Madonna (for whom Stephen still retains enormous respect and affection) convinced him that he was not making the type of films that he truly wanted to make.

In 2001, perhaps depressed and disillusioned with Hollywood, Stephen began his first book on spiritual cinema. He moved from Los Angeles to Oregon, where he finished the book. His first producer-director credit in independent spiritual cinema was *Indigo* (2003), starring Neale Donald Walsch. This was Stephen's foray into working exclusively in the spiritual cinema genre, which he earned the credit for recognizing and naming in his 2002 book, *The Force Is with You: Mystical Movie Messages That Inspire Our Lives*. By touring the country, hosting workshops, introducing people to spiritual cinema, and maintaining the connections he established Stephen brought the genre of spiritual cinema into the public forum. In this book that detailed more than seventy movies that best represented the genre, Stephen defined spiritual cinema as "a metaphoric pathway to explore such things as the nature of love, the meaning of life and death, the concept of time and space, and the visions of our future."

"Movies," Stephen believes, "are the most electrifying communications medium ever devised and the natural conduit of inspiring ourselves to look into the eternal issues of who we are and why we are here."

In a second book with Dr. Gay Hendricks, PhD, *Spiritual Cinema: A Guide to Movies That Inspire, Heal, and Empower Your Life*, published in 2005, Stephen and Gay expand the profiles of movies that matter and talk about the genesis of The Spiritual Cinema Circle, co-founded by Stephen and Gay, which began distributing spiritual films in the spring of 2004.

ERIC DELABARRE   ERIC DELABARRE   ERIC DELABARRE

Perhaps the question I hear most about writing this film is, "So, how do you adapt a book that is nothing more than a conversation of two voices and turn it into a movie?" Now, I could answer the question with all sorts of ego-driven replies like, "Because I'm good" or, "That's the beauty of being me." But the answer to the question is simply this—love. I do it by falling in love with what I'm doing, which is writing something that makes a difference.

Conversations with God came into my life because years ago I noticed that something was missing. I noticed that I wanted to love more deeply. I wanted to feel more deeply. When I began my journey to become a writer, something happened along the way. At first, I thought it was to become a famous writer (a runaway thought, courtesy of my ego). Then I thought I was on my way to becoming rich (greed to feed the ego). What really ended up happening along the way was that I became a man. When I walked away from a life on *Law & Order* because I was hungry for my own expression, my life began.

After writing my book *Why Not: Start Living Your Life Today* in 2003, I knew I wanted to continue on the path of making a difference in my own life. I guess, then, it's no mistake that I was watching *Jerry Maguire* on my laptop on the flight from L.A. to Medford in December 2004. When Jerry and Rod Tidwell decide to "risk everything and play out the season" and hope for a new contract, the flight captain made the following announcement over

Publicist Lisa Schneiderman and production attorney Cynthia Litman pose with Eric on the first day of principal photography

the intercom: "We're getting reports from Medford tower that the fog might be a problem. We need about one mile of visibility, and right now it's dancing right around that mark. Now, this could change any minute, but we're going to give it a try. If it's too thick, we'll need to land in Redding and bus you in."

My heart began to sink. All sorts of runaway thoughts began to race through my mind. Is this some sort of sign telling me that I won't get the job? I remember thinking, "Limited thinking gets limited results." I shut down my PowerBook and quickly grabbed my iPod because sometimes I think my life has a running score of music. I slowly closed my eyes, and right there on the plane, I began to pray. Now, I'm not one to beseech God and pray only when the yogurt hits the fan, but here I was praying. Not so much with an "Oh please, God" mantra, but in affirmation by repeating, "I will land in Medford, and I *am* the writer of *CWG* the movie. I will land in Medford, and I *am* the writer of *CWG* the movie." Over and over like the lines in a song I prayed. Then, it happened . . . the tires touched down on to the damp tarmac of Medford, Oregon.

I walked out of the gate to find the man who would become my friend and mentor on

Eric goes over the shooting schedule with videographer Ed Keller.

this project: producer/director Stephen Simon. The last time I saw Stephen was at Agape International Spiritual Center in Los Angeles. Stephen was giving one of the first of The Spiritual Cinema Circle presentations, and I remember thinking that I loved this man because he was standing not *against* something (Hollywood) but *for* something that would make a difference in peoples' lives (mostly his own). We got into his car, and he drove me directly to Neale's house. On the way, he told me how lucky I was to land. The writer they had interviewed yesterday had to land in Redding, California and take a six-hour bus ride to Ashland.

In about twenty-five minutes' time, I was walking up the steps of Neale's house. Surreal? Perhaps, but this was something I had asked for when I left network television. Here I was, meeting the writer of all these amazing books and being considered to adapt his works. It was perfect, I thought.

When I shook hands with Neale, I felt as if I was shaking hands with my brother. There was something going on. Something magical. We immediately sat down in his living room (which has an amazing view of the Rogue Valley) and the interview began. Neale asked what I thought the movie would be about. I remember saying something about the power of our

own intentions . . . and that God is moving through all of us . . . always . . . in all ways. We talked back and forth, and I could've kept it up for hours. There is something very exciting about talking with others who are actively making a difference in their own lives while also changing the lives of others. After about ten minutes, Neale looked over to Stephen and said, "If you don't mind, I'd like to stop here."

My heart sank. I felt like Jerry Maguire getting fired by Bob Sugar. Remember the brilliant fade where Jerry could hear the sounds of the ice cracking in his glass? I could hear my heart beating like a bass drum. The moisture in my mouth evaporated. How was this happening, I wondered. But this was nothing more than thoughts of lack and limitation because Neale continued his sentence, "This feels right. He's the guy."

They nodded to each other, and then Stephen said, "Great, let's get to work." I can see myself sitting in the chair when I heard this. I tried to be so cool as I pulled out my notebook. Oh yes, I was cool on the outside, but on the inside I wanted to shout in celebration. I remember saying to myself, "Prayer works because I *am* the writer of CWG the movie."

So it began. In January 2005, I met with Neale Donald Walsch, Stephen Simon, and the film's creative consultant, Viki King. They would become my "dream team" because together, everyone can achieve more. Yes, this is a cliché to some, but it is also the truth for everyone. I have relied too heavily on the self in the past. I am now trusting in others, without any limiting thoughts or fears of them stealing my idea. I could write for hours about the experience with my dream team of mentors, but I can sum the experience up in one word: Love (God).

After our first four-day intensive, I began the process of putting together a sort of dramatic structure for the film. The one thing I wanted to accomplish with the script was to somehow include the voice of God (from Book One) in all of the characters of the film. I wanted to show the audience that no person, despite circumstance or appearance, is void of God. Essentially, I wanted to showcase how God is all around us—all knowing and all loving.

The great thing about spending six years on *Law & Order* was being around Dick Wolf's emphasis on structure. "If it doesn't move the story forward, lose it." In order to make structural sense of Neale's life, I decided to write a linear outline first. Once the story beats were agreed upon, we would decide where the jumps to Book Neale and flashbacks to Homeless Neale would occur. Our main concern during this process was to make sure we didn't confuse the audience. If we lost the audience, the message would be lost as well. So we began to cut and paste the beats to the story, during which we lost (and gained) some scenes along the way. This is all part of the process of creating dramatic structure—rewriting. This process doesn't end with the script, as the next evolution of the script is the screen.

Sometimes the structure you have on paper doesn't work on screen. As a screenwriter, you have to accept this. I had to let go and allow that next evolution to take place. Essentially I had to "be mindful not to wish away *what is* by wanting *what is not*." That's a line I wrote for the character of Sunny. And although the line didn't make it into the film, it is the truth and a reminder for all of us. Sure, it's tough to let go when you write something, but that is part of growing up, becoming a man along the way, becoming a writer in love with God.

Eric DelaBarre
Santa Monica, California

Stephen says about Eric: "Even though I had talked to many writers over the years about possibly writing *CWG* if and when the rights were acquired, Eric was obviously the one destined to be the screenwriter. Eric added so much to the process with his fierce determination to make it the best script it could possibly be, and his passion compelled me to always be open to new possibilities. His sense of structure was crucial in that he never let us wander away from the narrative. He was fearless in trying new things, creating character profiles, and being the catalyst for huge shifts in direction. You simply cannot make any kind of a powerful film without a terrific script as its underpinning. Eric took an idea out of the ethers and gave it form, life, humor, and humanity."

Eric DelaBarre began his film career with Executive Producer Dick Wolf on NBC's hit

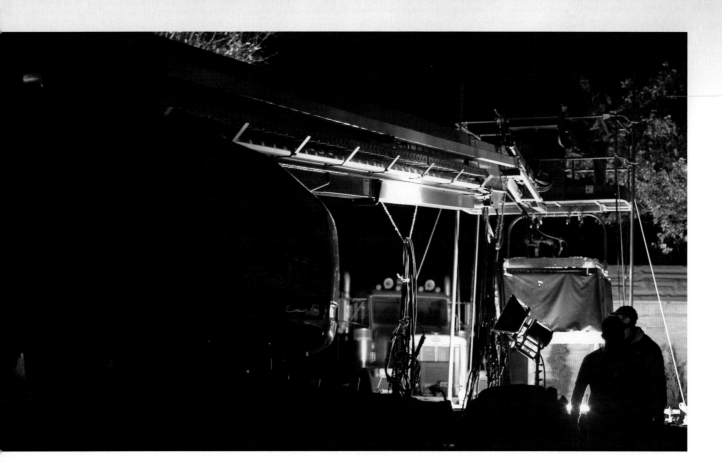

series *Law & Order*. Eric gained membership to the prestigious Writers Guild of America in 1997; and after six years at Wolf Films working on *Law & Order*, he decided to pursue a free-lance career as a writer/director. His national commercial "Stop the Cycle," written, produced, and directed for The American Lung Association, earned Eric a Best Director nomination for its Monitor Award. Eric also wrote two episodes for the short-lived USA Network series *The Big Easy*.

Moving on to independent feature films in 1999, Eric wrote, produced, and directed his debut film *Kate's Addiction*. The Newport Beach International Film Festival named Eric Filmmaker of the Future after its screening, and the film was eventually picked up by Lions Gate Entertainment. Eric's work has been seen on HBO, Cinemax, Showtime, Starz Encore, and the USA Network. Eric is also the author of the critically acclaimed book *Why Not: Start Living Your Life Today*, which has been endorsed by best-selling authors Mark Victor Hansen (*Chicken Soup*), John Gray (*Men Are From Mars, Women Are From Venus*), and *Publishers Weekly*, *Awareness Magazine*, and Dr. Michael Beckwith of the Agape International Spiritual Center. In addition to authoring the screenplay for *CWG*, Eric also served as the director of its second unit that shot many of the establishing scenes in the movie.

Gay Hendricks: Executive Producer

GAY HENDRICKS   GAY HENDRICKS   GAY HENDRICKS

Gay Hendricks responded differently from his Stanford University classmates in their psychotherapy class when the professor asked them what they intended to do with their doctoral degrees. While the others were intent on establishing private practices, Gay wondered how he could bring the mind-soul connection to the awareness of a large population, and not just a patient group. Gay had already become a meditator, and he explored the metaphysics of profound teacher-masters like J. Krishnamurti and Ramana Maharshi. Gay's first "delivery system" for putting life-changing ideas into the hands of a mass audience was his own literature, now some twenty books, including best sellers *Conscious Loving* and *The Corporate Mystic*.

As a person who appreciated films, Gay realized that movies provide a powerful potential for consciousness raising. The experience of a movie is immediate and it leaps over many barriers associated with social status. A film could be shown on a white sheet stretched between two jungle trees to an audience who could neither read nor write and still have impact.

Gay met Stephen Simon through mutual film industry friends when they were considering a screenplay that he had written. Over time, the two men attracted a synergy of people

*Gay and The Spiritual Cinema Circle President, Lisa Alderson, pause
on the Emigrant Lake location to engage screenwriter Eric DelaBarre.*

involved in the media and entertainment industry who were asking the same question: How can entertainment vehicles, like movies, be used for the betterment of the human condition? Gay suggested that many consciousness-raising films were already in existence, but that they languished for lack of attention in a commercially-dominated market. What if they could identify these films and offer them direct on DVD to a circle of subscribers? The manifestation of that drastic idea was the founding of The Spiritual Cinema Circle.

Stephen says: "Everyone should know that the idea for The Spiritual Cinema Circle was Gay's inspiration. Gay gave form to ideas about which I had only been dreaming for years. As a business partner, counselor, and dear friend, Gay has changed my life in more ways than I can ever enumerate. As a business partner, he is a visionary genius, pure and simple."

In the feature film production of *Conversations with God*, Circle members are in essence co-producers of the film. Their support of the Circle has made this independent production possible.

"There are not many books that have touched so many people," Gay says. "Adapting *Conversations* to film will expand its wisdom to even larger audiences."

Viki King: Consultant

Viki King was handed a copy of *Conversations with God* by publisher Bob Friedman at a national book convention when it was first published by Hampton Roads Publishing Company. Although she received many books that day, *Conversations with God* was the book that she read and instinctively "tabbed" with sticky notes as a way of structuring it for a movie. Then she put the book on a shelf and waited for all of the other forces to line up for actual production.

Viki was Stephen's confidante and adviser on every aspect of developing the *CWG* movie. She describes her role in this way: "Making a film is a metaphor. My job is to view the film from a soul level, to hold the light for how the cast and crew can function as a team."

About Stephen, she says, "Stephen is a gatherer of the tribe. And the tribe hears him, and there is an instant remembrance. He has a way of busting people's hearts wide open when they are so longing to give their gifts. People are willing to take the creative leap with a sense of urgency. Stephen says to them, 'We are the ones we have been waiting for.' Stephen awakens and inspires people to initiate their own projects, not just participate in his. The big picture is the fitting together of all the puzzle pieces represented by everyone's personal hopes, dreams, and aspirations. Everyone is an equal part of the grand design."

About Gay Hendricks, Viki says, "Gay has so many areas of expertise. He has entered into deep agreement on what our shared vision is. He can also dot all the organizational *is* and cross all the business *ts*. That kind of integration is very positive."

Viki was very impressed with Henry Czerny's performance as Neale. En route to start work on the film, Viki and Henry shared a plane ride to Ashland. "When we saw Mt. Shasta out the plane window we decided to do a ceremony, knowing that everyone who has come to participate in the making of the film has climbed their own personal mountain to get there. Together we now go forward to our collective destiny. Henry's performance was impeccable and he is a lovely dear man."

Viki felt a special bonding to Ingrid Boulting, who held the role of Sunny. "The scene in Sunny's trailer is so important for all of us to move into the Divine Feminine. This film allows men to become grownups and [to] step into their manhood. Women have the choice to relate to men as men, not boys. They are not to be their mothers, or their healers, or to fix it or solve it. They are not to be invested. They can be there as full, powerful women to allow for a man to choose for himself if he wishes to step into his manhood."

Viki states, "We had Sunny, as the Oracle, say, 'Heal that and you will be free.' This sentence encodes for the cast and the crew and those watching the film the possibility of their personal transcendence. I whole-heartedly acknowledge the enormous power from the first string Goddesses working on the film for their considerable bravery in stepping up. They lovingly held the light. The Divine Feminine is dawned. This creates the Divine Feminine for men to be fully men, for women to be fully women, and for all of us in full partnership to step forward in the power of being our whole selves. Imagine that! This film opens the space for that understanding. It reaches people where they are and offers them the opportunity to take the next step."

Since the publication of her book *How to Write a Movie in 21 Days: The Inner Movie Method* in 1988, Viki has been in demand as a lecturer and a workshop speaker all over the world. Viki has been a creative consultant for and offers wise counsel to many high profile clients from world leaders to Hollywood icons.

Viki King and Eric DelaBarre are two of the most talented people I know. My admiration for them both grew fast and strong during the days of our collaboration.

Viki is deeply intuitive, and when you add that to her other strengths and skills, she brings to the business of building a story for film an uncanny knack for knowing where the basement is. Everyone else is looking at the visible structure of the story while Viki is looking underground, digging, digging, until she finds the treasure buried beneath the basement. Not *in* the basement, *beneath* the basement.

If the screenwriter's job is to flesh out a story, Viki's gift is locating the skeleton. What do you put the flesh *on*? That is always Viki's question. Through this Viki finds motivations, mental frameworks, and emotional content that no one else might have guessed was there, deeply impacting and richly enhancing the original "plot" by revealing the real story that wants to emerge. That is exactly how Viki looks at it, by the way. "Wait, wait," she would say at scripting conferences. "There's a larger story here that wants to emerge."

Eric, for his part, has the unique ability of synthesization. Is that a word? It is now. Webster defines *synthesis* as "the composition or combination of parts or elements so as to form a whole." Indeed. Eric can synthesize anything. He can take a bagful of memories and turn it into a handful of experiences (which is all that a movie can hold), capturing the essence and the wonder and the naked, raw truth of the larger reality and squeezing it into our minds in *one hundred minutes of script*.

Whoa. That, my friends, is not easy.

Stephen talks about Viki: "No words can ever come close to describing how much Viki has meant to *CWG* and me, both personally and as a director/producer. Without Viki, this film could not have become anything close to what it is. She was our spiritual collaborator all the way through the process, and when things got challenging for any of us, Viki was always there to lovingly guide us. It is so difficult to actually put into words who Viki is and how she has so impacted both the film and all of our lives. For instance, she introduced me to the whole notion of the Divine Feminine energy which surrounds the film, but [it] is so hard to actually find the word to explain how she did that. She indeed 'is' that energy and she finds the most loving and compassionate ways to communicate that to everyone. Her shamanic wisdom, insights, and compassion are reflected on every frame of the film and are forever etched in my heart and soul."

Stephanie Angel, script supervisor says about Viki: "We all made a sacred contract to come together at this particular time and place in life, a time outside of time to connect and create this powerful story into a film so that the truth may shine bright. This is just the beginning . . . and it is so beautiful to be here now. I want to thank Viki for collecting the Goddesses and for holding the sacred energy on set. Viki stands up in her highest power for the intangible necessities that often get overlooked. That is the power of love manifested."

Lisa Alderson: President, Cinema Circle, Inc.

LISA ALDERSON   LISA ALDERSON   LISA ALDERSON

Lisa Alderson is an entrepreneur who has always been interested in the potential of media. In high school and college she was active in radio and television production. In college, she founded CTV, a television station affiliated with Colorado State University that is now one of the top student-run stations in the country. Early in her career, Lisa produced television documentaries. She was also an intern at CBS News but was not fulfilled by the "heaviness" of news journalism. She was creative and had a passion for building projects that mattered by promoting social and attitudinal changes.

After receiving an MBA at Harvard, Lisa contributed to long-term strategy planning at Disney, ABC, and CNN. She then returned to her entrepreneurial roots and started several companies at the cross-section of media and technology. From these experiences Lisa asked herself, "What can I do with media, entertainment, and technology to change society?" She found her answer when she was introduced to Stephen Simon and Gay Hendricks at a meeting of The Spiritual Cinema Circle in Ojai, California.

As the staff of the Circle continued to develop, it was evident that the contributing members were very different individuals who came from separate experiences but who arrived at the same place in time with the same purpose and mutual immediate recognition of each

other's skill levels and spiritual depth. Further, all members could see the potential to raise the consciousness on the planet via entertainment.

On the set of *CWG* Lisa witnessed the fruition of her ardent desire to make the world a better place through creative initiatives. Her joy was magnified in the knowledge of a future gift that would be presented to the four-month-old son that she and husband David shared—Owen. The legacy of Lisa's work today would result in her son's reality of tomorrow.

Cynthia Litman: Production Attorney

CYNTHIA LITMAN   CYNTHIA LITMAN   CYNTHIA LITMAN

Cynthia Litman is the attorney for The Spiritual Cinema Circle and its related businesses and the production attorney for *CWG*. She's been involved with *CWG* from the onset and has completely devoted her legal career to spiritual entertainment. Her mother and spiritual mentor, Gail, says that from the age of twelve Cynthia had a career focus—she wanted to meet and work for Steven Spielberg! She held this focus through college as a pre-law major and a psychology and theatrical arts minor, and in law school, where she studied entertainment law. Guideposts to a career as a spiritual entertainment attorney included internships at a New York talent agency and a Pittsburgh recording studio, three years working with an independent film producer/attorney while attending New York Law School, and four years in the business and legal affairs department at New Line Cinema.

Cynthia's spiritual sensitivity led her to attend Stephen Simon's New York 2002 workshop entitled *Insights and Intrigue – A Producer's Perspective on Filmmaking*. Stephanie Angel, the film's eventual script supervisor, also attended this workshop and sat in front of Cynthia. She admits that she had seen only one Stephen Simon-produced film, the family favorite *Bill & Ted's Excellent Adventure*. She now affectionately refers to Stephen as the "Royal Ugly Dude."

Cynthia on set with (left to right) her father Larry, script supervisor
Stephanie Angel, husband Craig, and Eric DelaBarre.

"Yes, what a lovely tribute," smiles Stephen. "Cynthia came in to spiritual cinema and my life with wisdom and judgment way beyond her years. There is no one in the world that I trust more than Cynthia."

After attending Stephen's workshop, corresponding with him, and taking his telecourse, Cynthia established a deep connection with Stephen, and she decided to abandon her child-to-adulthood moviemaking fixation on Steven Spielberg. Stephen Simon was close enough!

Cynthia was only 27 years old, but meeting Stephen clearly was a shining guidepost to her pathway. She helped Stephen build a community of individuals dedicated to making entertainment more meaningful. With Stephen, Cynthia has found a creative cause that has fired her imagination and enabled her to utilize all of her talents, skills, and education with her spirituality intact.

The impetus of being involved with spiritually-relevant films brought Cynthia, Stephen, and Gay and Kathlyn Hendricks to a table at the Morning Glory Restaurant in Ashland. There they joined their talents to manifest a radical new idea: a membership DVD club for the direct distribution of movies that matter. By April 2004, The Spiritual Cinema Circle was launched with the distribution of a selection of spiritual films. In May 2005, the Transformational Book Circle was incorporated.

Cynthia sees and treasures her role as the protector of Stephen and the Circle, and as the bridge builder between the creative and business aspects of the entertainment industry. The Circle's business policy is to be transparent, and Cynthia aims to uphold the values of honesty and integrity in all of her business dealings.

Cynthia first met Muriel Stockdale, *CWG*'s costume designer, through one of Stephen's first telecourses. They later teamed up to co-found ISE-NY (The Institute for Spiritual Entertainment-New York).

On the set of *CWG*, Cynthia was accompanied by husband Craig Kugel, mother Gail, and father Larry. Since the senior Litmans have always honored and supported Cynthia's focus on entertainment, it was appropriate that they got to witness and participate in the realization of her dream. Being a soft drink distributor for more than thirty years, Larry was aptly cast in the film as Truck Driver while the other Litmans landed background roles in the film, making Stephen wonder if he missed any Litmans. Cynthia's beloved sister, Valerie, vowed not to miss the next film!

Joao Fernandes: Director of Photography

JOAO FERNANDES   JOAO FERNANDES   JOAO FERNANDES

Joao Fernandes has more than fifty filmography credits as a cinematographer dating from 1975 and including feature films, TV movies, and TV series. Three times in the 1990s, Joao directed episodes of *Walker, Texas Ranger*. Joao is a native of Rio de Janeiro, Brazil, but he has lived in the U.S. for the last thirty-five years: first in New York where he attended NYU Film School, then in Los Angeles, and today in Ashland. As a director of photography, Joao has worked in Europe, Africa, the Middle East, Asia, and the U.S. He photographed *One Man's Hero* with Tom Berenger, *Gideon's Web* with Charlton Heston and Carroll O'Connor, and *Road to Galveston* with Cicely Tyson and Piper Laurie, to note a few accomplishments.

About Joao Fernandes, Viki King says, "Joao was able to be in on all our script development meetings, which is not common. He is a precious man with so much expertise in his area. He is very thoughtful, so when he speaks in a meeting, he is brilliant. He has the frame of each scene elegantly thought out before he gives advice. It was Stephen's idea to involve Joao almost ten months prior to filming, so we got his valuable input at every stage."

Stephen says, "Joao was an integral collaborator on *CWG*. As a director, it was crucial to have a director of photography whom I could trust and also who would be patient with my

sometimes unintelligible attempts at describing how things might look. Having worked together on *Indigo* gave Joao and me the opportunity to establish that trust, and it reached new levels on *CWG*. We had the luxury in prep of spending several weeks looking at reference films together so that we could create just the look we wanted for the film. Most importantly, Joao passionately loves what he does; and, as a result, he was always anticipating everything before it happened and, at the same time, was able to create a look for the film that gives new definition to beauty in HD (high definition). He is also one of the kindest, warmest, and most wonderful people in the world. He will be the cinematographer on every film I ever do."

I've talked about some of the other members of the initial creative team earlier, but I didn't have much to say there about Joao—even though he played a key role in creative decisions right from the start . . . and well he should have.

Joao Fernandes is one of the most extraordinary people I have ever met. He has an incredible eye for what I want to call "the artistry of life." That is what makes him a wonderful choice as the director of photography for any film. He is an extremely sensitive man (who hates to have that revealed and who, in truth, cannot help but show it) with a gentle irony of expression that provokes sweet laughter. His kindness of heart is evident in everything he says and does, and washes over all those he touches. He is simply a lovely, lovely human being, the kind of man you would walk a hundred miles for and feel honored to have done so. This film was blessed to have his talent, and even more blessed to have his presence. My life is immeasurably enriched by knowing him and calling him my friend.

Casting

CASTING   CASTING   CASTING

The casting process for the supporting and featured extra roles in *CWG* involved a five-day marathon open casting call at the Ashland Springs Hotel in late August 2005. Non-union auditions were held on Monday for women and on Tuesday for men. SAG (Screen Actors Guild) auditions were held on Wednesday for men and Thursday for women with final callbacks scheduled for Friday. The workdays, organized by casting director Kathy Wilson, went from 8 AM to 6 PM. Prospective cast members could go to The Spiritual Cinema Circle website for character breakdowns and even to download sides (specific character dialogue) or scenes in which their chosen characters had dialogue.

Hopefuls who had followed the progress of the movie in development through membership in The Spiritual Cinema Circle (where they received monthly *Behind the Seen* video diaries produced for the Circle by Edify Productions), who had completed workshops with Stephen, or who visited Neale's website made plans to come from all over the U.S. to audition. Many of these people were not professional actors, but their passion to participate in the making of the movie was undeniable. And so, in something very rare in feature film casting, the first two days of the auditions were given over to unproven talent with the full participation of the director and the subject himself, Neale Donald Walsch.

Kathy Wilson has a talent agency background, taught "Agents and Acting" to college students, and was introduced to Stephen Simon by mutual friends in Los Angeles. In a casting call placed on the L.A. website Breakdown she yielded six hundred responses for the Carly role alone.

Prior to founding her own film production company, WaveLink Productions, Kathy was

Laurie Farley on set with casting find, actor Jerry McGill.

a major player in the Portland, Oregon filmmaking, media, and advertising community. WaveLink is now in development of the feature film *Song of the Stone*, which is adapted from the book by Barry Brailsford. The film will be shot in New Zealand with Kathy as its primary producer.

Kathy says that she could have been fired as a casting manager on most other films for not pre-screening the long lines of amateur applicants, but Stephen insisted on meeting every-one who came. Auditioners for *CWG* received an opportunity to express themselves in a very gracious, non-judgmental environment.

For Stephen and Neale, the entire casting process was about relationships. Instead of pro-ducing anxiety and disappointment, the spirit of the experience created a sense of joyful collaboration as more than forty supporting and feature roles were cast, along with some thirty featured extras. One of these personal encounters led to a small speaking role for a woman known only as Suki. She had bonded with other women on the 2005 Spiritual Cinema Festival-at-Sea, a film festival hosted by The Spiritual Cinema Circle, and had been aided in her healing from cancer by them. Suki can be seen as the radiant woman wearing the head scarf in the New Age Church scene.

Assigned to screen applicants at the *CWG* open casting call, casting assistant Laurie Farley, who worked on the production of *Indigo* and also spearheaded efforts to get spiritual cinema in video stores everywhere, met Jerry McGill, a quadriplegic who obviously did not match the script description of the character Oscar. Oscar was thought to be more like a retired Army drill sergeant. Laurie, however, bravely asked the casting decision makers to consider Jerry, and they changed their concept of the role when they met him. On set, Laurie acted as Jerry's assistant and dialogue coach.

Laurie also immediately recognized Zillah Glory as the film's Carly and sent her to the head of the audition line. She was cast the same day. Laurie is currently moving toward more extensive developmental roles in spiritual cinema films.

If there is a more electric day on a movie project than the start of casting, I'd like to know what it is. There are many that are *as* charged (like the first day of shooting, or a big special effects day, or the day on which a hugely important scene is going to be shot, or Wrap Day), but none more so than Casting Day, I don't think.

I was *so* excited when I arrived at the hotel. People were lined up outside the place, some having been there since early morning. I'd gone over to Stephen's place (he and I both make Ashland our home) to pick him up, and he flashed me a huge smile as he slipped into the Prius. "Well, bro," he chirped. "This is it! Here we go! Today it's real!"

I felt just as exhilarated as he did. We laughed and joked and just talked as I drove the few blocks that we had to go (everything is seven minutes from everything else in Ashland). When we got to the hotel and saw all those people leaning against the building, Stephen turned into a kid. "Let's work the line!" he said. "Let's tell 'em how terrific it is for them to have come and how much we appreciate it!"

So we did. We parked in the lot behind the hotel, came around the corner, and surprised everybody in line by introducing ourselves and shaking hands. We asked them about themselves, how far they had come, what drove them to it, and all the neat things you talk about on a fine summer morning when you're about to cast a feature film.

We posed on the sidewalk for a few pictures, and then went inside to chat with the production staff already assembled and set about the task we'd come to do. The final decision on all casting would be Stephen's, of course, but he invited me to sit at his side throughout the auditions. He never failed to ask my opinion.

Now, I've been involved in enough professional and semi-professional the-atre (with more than forty-five years as an actor, producer, and director) to know that auditions can be a brutal process of abrupt cut-offs, bruised egos, and less than cordial let's-get-on-with-it efficiency. Not so here. Stephen did everything he could to make the next person coming into the room feel as relaxed as possible. He never once cut an actor's reading short (even when he and everyone else in the room knew that the reading was not good enough to merit a call back) and never, ever failed to end the audition with kind and com-plimentary words. He found something good to say to *everyone* without ever reducing himself to being disingenuous or inauthentic.

Stephen was determined to maintain the dignity of both the actors and the process—never allowing it to even get close to being what it could so easily be: dehumanizing. I admire him so much for that. He was going to have none of this "show business is tough" stuff, and those who auditioned for him deeply appreciated it. You could see it on their faces as they left.

The auditions were held in a small conference room on the second floor of the hotel, with a video camera planted in the corner and a couple of small tables filling one end and behind which sat Stephen, myself, and casting direc-tor Kathy Wilson. A few others came and went during the five days of casting, but we three were there for all of it. Many of the auditions were truly spectac-ular, and after each such one we would all sit there for a beat in stunned silence. Then Stephen would say, "The gods are smiling. The gods are smiling."

And, indeed, they were.

For me this business of casting was another part of the whole program that bordered on the surreal. These actors entered the room one after the other, pretending for a moment to be people that I know! While, as I mentioned ear-lier, some of the roles were composite characters, not all of them were. So there I was, sitting there watching people portray people who actually *peopled my life.*

But the most mind-bending moment of all was when young Zillah Glory came in to audition for the part of Carly (the role she was eventually given). The person who was reading against our auditioners was temporarily out of the room, so to keep the process moving, I offered to sit in and read the part of "me." Are you ready for this? I mean, *think about it.* And don't think *that* wasn't weird. Reading from a *movie* script the part of *yourself* against an actress por-traying a scene from your own life???? *Come on!*

Henry Czerny (as Neale Donald Walsch)

HENRY CZERNY   HENRY CZERNY   HENRY CZERNY

I wanted to be involved in *CWG* because of the material. When I read the script and then the book, I recognized that they were a compilation of what I had myself been thinking; and here it was, beautifully written in a concise and simple way that I could now use to model my personal thoughts. As a storyteller, I want to be involved in projects that give voice to my passions, and in *CWG*, I saw a story that has been waiting to be told for centuries.

I think this story will connect with people in the unique way that a mountain, heaved onto the horizon millenniums ago, is experienced by a wayfarer from the prairie. Undeniably tangible, universal, and true. We all respond intrinsically to nature because it is about who we are, not as one individual or a hero, but who we are collectively.

I don't think that there has ever been a time in our history when inspirational messages have not been essential to our evolutionary process. In *Conversations with God*, Neale is able to make a sense of his journey for all of us. He is able to understand what he went through and why. But his journey is also ours. This is what makes *CWG*, the movie journey, absolutely extraordinary. In the end, it is extraordinarily inclusive.

Henry Czerny
Los Angeles, California

More than a month after filming, Henry said from his home in Los Angeles, "The experience of making *CWG* reverberates daily without signs of diminishing in my consciousness. Its effect is more embracing and, oddly, more challenging every day. Making *Conversations* is proving to be a seminal place in the timeline of my life."

"There are not enough adjectives in the world to describe Henry, both as an actor and as a human being," says Stephen. "The role of playing Neale in *CWG* was an incredibly demanding one. First of all, with the exception of three brief moments, Henry is present in every scene in the film. The character goes from being homeless to being very successful, so the character arc is as steep as one can imagine. To add to that challenge, he also is playing a real-life person.

"Henry hit every moment without ever missing a beat. His performance is beyond extraordinary. Even more so, he was always willing to go the extra mile—in every shot, in every scene, for the film, for his own character, and for all the other actors. His generosity of spirit to his fellow actors became one of the linchpins of the performances in the film. When you see Henry play this role, you are watching the real artistry of acting taken to its most sublime levels.

"If there is indeed any match to Henry the actor, it is Henry the man. I consider myself the luckiest guy in the world to have been able to spend those weeks with him. Just as he is a consummate pro as an actor, so is he as a human being. Unfailingly kind, positive, loving, warm, and compassionate, Henry has absolutely none of the ego airs that infiltrate much of the Hollywood film business. I will cherish our collaboration and friendship for the rest of my life."

Henry Czerny is a native of Toronto, Canada and was trained in its National Theatre School, where he is now regarded as one of its most respected dramatic actors. Since his breakthrough portrayal in the CBC-produced miniseries *The Boys of St. Vincent*, for which he won a 1994 Best Actor Canadian Gemini Award, Henry has worked constantly in feature films and television dramas. Henry was the clever CIA chief opposite Harrison Ford in *Clear and Present Danger* (1994) and his impressive film credits include *Notes From Underground* (1995), *Mission Impossible* (1996), *The Ice Storm* (1997), *Kayla* (1998), *The Exorcism of Emily Rose* (2005), *Fido* (2006), and *The Pink Panther* (2006).

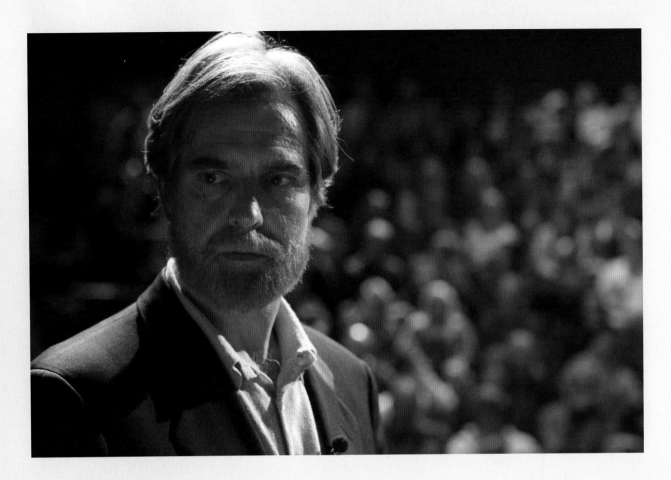

Of course, my biggest interest was in who would be cast as Movie Neale. When it turned out to be Henry Czerny, I was absolutely delighted. I had seen Henry's work in other films, and I knew him to be a fine actor. What made me happiest, though, was Stephen's revelation to me that Henry is "really in harmony with the material."

It isn't every day that you stand by and watch a man cast in the role of *you* in a feature film. I know I keep harping on this, but you have to understand what an extraordinary situation this is. I found that I had a lot more emotional baggage around this casting choice than I expected to have. You certainly don't want a person playing "you" who cannot find a genuine place of agreement inside of himself with who you are as a person, and with what you deeply believe. (If you were Bill Clinton, you probably would not want Rush Limbaugh to play you on film!) So I was relieved to learn that Henry agreed with much of what I had written in *Conversations with God*. And it didn't hurt that he was movie star handsome. (After all, we do want to get as close to the original as possible, right?)

I finally met Henry at the Ashland Springs Hotel. Stephen had asked me to stop by so that we could meet and have a chat. As I approached the hotel I saw Henry in full make-up as "Neale, the street person" leaning against the building, next to the front door. I could not believe how much like me he really *did* look, particularly in profile.

Inside the lobby we sat and talked for about thirty minutes, and that was the last I saw of him in person until the second-to-last day of shooting. I've done a lot of acting in my life, a tiny bit on film, a ton of it in regional and dinner theatres around the country, and I know something about the actor's art. One thing I would never want to have to do is play the role of a living person *who is standing right in front of me.* It's tough enough playing the part of a fictional character, much less a real person to whom everyone is going to compare me later. It would be completely unfair to ask me as an actor to be subjected to such comparisons right in the moment that I am trying to create a role. There was no way I was going to allow that to happen to Henry. Stephen, of course, was way ahead of me on this, and so we were in agreement that I would not visit the set during principal shooting.

As for Henry, he had already decided, as any good actor would, that he had no intention of doing an impersonation of me. Rather, he would create a portrayal of me as he, the actor, felt it. Having said that it is uncanny how close to me in mannerisms and appearance he came in certain scenes. Everyone who knows me well says so (one of my children, after seeing the film, said, "God, I have seen that exact look on Dad's face"), and even I have to admit that in some moments Henry's portrayal is *freaky* close.

The final night of shooting I returned to the set to thank Henry and to say goodbye. I felt, in a way that fascinated me, that we had been through a bonding experience together. Here was a man who had poured himself into the role of *me,* who had lived through, in as realistic a way as an actor can manage (and Henry is a very *good* actor), the same experiences I'd lived through. And, unlike me, *he* did it all in a series of highly intense emotional encounters jammed into six weeks!

He and I stood there on the final night of shooting and just looked into each other's eyes for a moment, not saying anything. There was really nothing that words could add to what our eyes conveyed. *Thank you, brother. Thank you.* Both ways.

Vilma Silva (as Leora)

Stephen saw Vilma in a production of the Oregon Shakespeare Festival (OSF), where she has played major roles since 1994. "I invited Vilma to audition, but that was really just a formality," Stephen says. "From the moment I saw her command the stage in *Gibraltar*, the play in which she was starring at the time, I already knew that she would play Leora, the primary woman's role in *CWG*. Vilma has a unique combination of brilliant talent, beauty, wit, and strength that just bursts off the screen. She is also the consummate pro. In every scene, she was always letter-perfect from take one on and is truly a director's dream."

Although she had never met Stephen, one of Vilma's all-time favorite movie scenes is from his film *What Dreams May Come*, when the Robin Williams' character first gets to heaven and is greeted by his dog. Vilma hopes to see her dearly departed pet in the same way.

In her relationship with Neale, the character Leora realizes the compromises that she has made in her own life, and through this her awareness of self is raised. Vilma sees a parallel. Although university trained in theatre, Vilma spent seven years in the banking field before she realized that job security was a poor choice if it required her to subdue her passion for acting. Vilma wanted a higher sense of living. While reading *Conversations with God*, she asked,

"What is it that would be your heaven?" For her it was the arts. Now, as an actress in spiritual cinema, Vilma sees her horizons expanding to even greater levels of experience. "We're taking the 'middle man' out of our relationship with God," she says.

This role is a composite character, and Vilma played it wonderfully well. There are several people in my life who will see themselves in this character. The generous lady who typed my first manuscript practically for free (I think I gave her $15 here and there) is one of them. I will never forget her kindness, and she receives a small portion of the royalties from *Conversations with God, Book One* to this very day. My events scheduler, Rita Curtis, who showed up at more than one out-of-town location to lend a hand, is another. And the wonderful lady whom I married after that first book contract was signed and who did all that traveling to book signings and lectures, is a third. Nancy stood by me and looked on from the sidelines, just as Leora does on screen, offering me physical and emotional support during the hectic tours and times that are dramatized in the movie.

Again, if we had introduced these "characters" from my life separately, we would have had to tell a far lengthier story, and the focus of the film would have made it feel very much like a "bio pic"—exactly what we did not want. So we strayed from the true-life story line just a bit, scrunched three people into Leora, and managed both to keep our film at a manageable length and to preserve the privacy of personal moments between husband and wife.

On set, Vilma was impressed with the generosity of both cast and crew. Trained in stagecraft, Vilma appreciated Stephen's sensitivity to her in adapting to the close-up camera. Henry, too, she says, was especially helpful to her in the handling of props for the close-ups.

On stage, in addition to starring roles at the Oregon Shakespeare Festival, Vilma has performed in Birmingham and London, England; at the La Jolla Playhouse in San Diego; at Actors Theatre of Louisville; Dallas Theatre Center; The Group Theatre (Seattle); and the American Conservatory Theatre among others. On television, she has been featured in movies for the Hallmark Hall of Fame and NBC.

Bruce Page (as Fitch)

A lot of actors wanted to be in this film because they had read the *Conversations with God* books and wanted to be associated with bringing its wisdom to the movie-going public. Bruce had attended a workshop with Stephen Simon that resulted in an ongoing friendship, and he had the right look and the acting credentials to play the pivotal role of Fitch, a homeless man who troubles Neale into a new reality.

Bruce shows a great sensitivity to the trials of emotion and doubt. He earned these insights as the parent of a seriously ill child. Stephen Simon never auditioned or even considered anyone else for the role of Fitch, and the character itself was written strictly with Bruce in mind.

Stephen says: "When we all met in January 2005 to discuss the character that would turn out to be Fitch, Bruce immediately came to my mind, and we developed everything about the character for him from that point forward. I called Bruce to tell him that we were developing a role for him—but I'm not sure he quite believed me! Bruce is one of those great, unsung heroes of the film industry. A brilliant actor, the quintessential chameleon who is constantly thinking, feeling, and intuiting new shades of depth for each moment. After we sent him the first draft, Bruce sent me a detailed analysis of everything about Fitch: his background, what brought him to the park—everything. His on-screen camaraderie with Neale is crucial to the film, and we couldn't have done the film without Bruce in that role."

Bruce is a bi-coastal actor who has been working out of Boston and Los Angeles for the last fifteen years. He has done off-Broadway stage roles as well as a memorable ESPN spot commercial for the initial *Extreme Games*. Clint Eastwood cast Bruce in *Mystic River* (2003), and he also held a starring role in *Ring of the Bishop* (2004) and a feature role in the Showtime series *Brotherhood/The Hill*.

On working with the director, Bruce says, "Stephen has a compassion that you pick up on. He is self-deprecating. He holds nothing back. He is a very talented individual who is capable of the kind of vulnerability that allows access to his life. That attribute gives actors a sense of security and allows us to express our innermost feelings. When he first saw me on the set, he greeted me with his usual warmth and enthusiasm. 'Do you believe me now?' Stephen said. 'We're actually doing it!'"

I spent an afternoon with Bruce at the camp site location on the day they were striking the set, and it was one of my most emotional experiences connected to this movie. The set was unbelievable, right down to the last detail. And Bruce, having played several scenes there as a street person, had a real flavor of what I had gone through in real life. We walked the set together, talking quietly about . . . well, about life, really . . . just talking about life more than about the movie. Then he stood by as the crew invited me to take down the first piece of the set—the tent where I lived while I was there. For me it was almost therapeutic. I got to visit my past, in a sense, and symbolically disassemble that very difficult time when I was living outside with no roof over my head and no place to call home other than that tent. Bruce and I shared a very special moment that day, and I fell in love with the guy. I also just love the work he did in this movie. What a completely believable portrayal.

Ingrid Boulting (as Sunny)

INGRID BOULTING   INGRID BOULTING   INGRID BOULTING

Ingrid Boulting brings a hauntingly spiritual presence to the pivotal role of Sunny. Twenty years ago, with a young daughter, Ingrid left a career as a star-status actor to begin a spiritual transformation that involved the practice and teaching of yoga and fine art painting. When she was first suggested for the role of Sunny, she backed away, not wanting to return to what she had experienced in previous moviemaking. Ingrid, however, had read the *Conversations with God* books, and soon she was in a dialogue with Stephen Simon about the different nature of spiritual cinema.

Stephen says, "Ingrid plays such a crucial role in the film, not just from the standpoint of acting, but also from a place of 'being-ness.' Sunny is not on the screen for very long, but her role is utterly pivotal in reshaping both Neale's self-perception and also his destiny. When I heard from Ingrid, I was truly floored. I knew she had left the business decades before, and I remembered her very well. She had just the perfect balance of mystery and presence to actually *be* Sunny, not just play her. We are all incredibly honored that Ingrid chose CWG as her return to films."

In the same way that the practice of yoga gives back what you give, Ingrid was moved by how the *CWG* script demonstrated the letting go of the layers of our lives. She sees the film as recognizing the fears inherent in the material world and then encouraging the viewer to make a step that solidifies a commitment to the spiritual journey. "We have landed," she says. "We are grounded."

Art, for Ingrid, is the journey of seeing, not unlike a motion picture, as a series of pictures. When she left Hollywood, it was "a jump into the unknown," but now it feels like no time has passed. "I felt the purpose when I came to work on *CWG*," she says. "My father was a filmmaker, but I saw it as a business rather than an art form. Ultimately, I was not being offered roles that matched my heart's desire."

"I see Sunny as Viki King, someone who is here to help us take the next step with love and wisdom. Sunny has been through a lot, so she understands Neale and she recognizes Neale as someone ready to make a giant step in transformation. She is saying, like Ram Dass, 'be here now.'"

"What can I say about Stephen? He is an actor's dream of patience and trust."

Ingrid Boulting spent her early childhood in South Africa. At age fifteen, she was discovered as a fashion model by *Bazaar Magazine*. Her photos appear in the great Richard Avedon books of photography. By age eighteen, Ingrid was an actress touring in repertory with the Oxford Playhouse. She has performed on stage, in television, and in films with such actors as Orson Welles, Laurence Harvey, Olivia de Havilland, and Nicole Williamson. She played opposite Robert De Niro in *The Last Tycoon* (1976).

Zillah Glory (as Carly)

Zillah Glory saw the *Indigo* before-film discussion with Stephen Simon, Neale Donald Walsch, and James Twyman and knew that she wanted to work with them. Zillah holds a theatre degree from the University of Minnesota and her goal as a performer is to "make things for people that will give them their hearts." Without a base, Zillah was on the road working for theatre companies and improving her craft when she learned about the open audition for *CWG*. Friends thought that she was crazy to travel from the East Coast to the West Coast to attend the audition. Her finances were so restricted that she had to sleep on the sofa of friends in Eugene, Oregon, and then make the long commute to Ashland. Zillah says that she had to "give up wanting the role of Carly" and focus on her intention to participate in spiritual cinema.

Casting screener Laurie Farley saw something special in Zillah and sent her immediately to read for Stephen. Zillah was surprised to find Neale in the room, and was a bit awed to shake his hand. Her mother had told her to read the *Conversations with God* series much earlier. Now here was Neale himself reading a scene from the screenplay with her. Stephen had not wanted her to prepare the scene because he wanted to experience the flow of her spontaneous energy. Stephen was so convinced that he had his Carly that he circumvented the usual call-back procedure and had Zillah read a second time the same day.

"We had over six hundred actress submissions for the role of Carly, and Zillah was the very first one to actually read for the role," says Stephen. "You know how, in the Olympics, you want to perform last so the judges have seen everyone else before you? Well, Zillah comes in, blows the part out of the water on a cold reading, and I'm sitting there thinking—what do I say to the other 599? Obviously, we went on with an open mind to read several other Carlys, but Zillah was an impossible act for anyone else to follow. She is a natural-born star with charisma to burn. I think of her as Lucille Ball and Reese Witherspoon combined into one person. What a career this young lady is going to have!"

Zillah is the eldest of seven children raised by a very courageous mother who allowed Zillah to choose her middle name at the age of seven. She chose Glory. Zillah worked her way through college, and she remains fearless in the pursuit of her art form. After appearing in *CWG*, she returned to work at the Charlotte Repertory Theatre in North Carolina and then moved on to Washington, D.C., where she is pursuing a master's degree at The Academy for Classical Acting.

Abdul Salaam El Razzac (as Chef)

Abdul is a tall, look-you-in-the-eyes kind of man with an unforgettable face. On Veterans Day 2005, he greeted another veteran of the Vietnam War era in his *CWG* set trailer and talked seriously about their common experience. Abdul can play Shakespearian characters as easily as he can play down-and-out men from his childhood neighborhood in St. Paul, Minnesota. His presence and range as an actor has been seen on television in *Star Trek: The Next Generation*, *General Hospital*, *Becker*, and *Frasier*, and in such feature films as *Pretty Woman*, *Glory*, *Malcolm X*, *Terminator 2: Judgment Day*, and more.

On the stage, Abdul was a founding member of the African-American Penumbra Theatre in St. Paul. In Los Angeles, he won the DramaLogue Award for Best Director of Oliver Mayer's *Joe Louis Blues* and a Drama Critics Award for his performance as Toledo in *Ma Rainey's Black Bottom*.

Fortunately for the production of *CWG*, Abdul was available in Ashland, playing that same character of Toledo in the OSF production of *Ma Rainey*.

"Having OSF here in Ashland was a gold mine of acting talent for us," says Stephen. "In 2005, I saw every play at OSF, consciously looking for actors to fill roles in *CWG*. Joao and I actually went to see *Ma Rainey* together. Ten minutes into the play, I turned to Joao and, referring to Abdul, I said, 'Well, that's Chef!'

"Abdul came aboard right away, not just as Chef, but as a trusted friend and ally. He helped me find other actors for *CWG* and even sat in on many of the auditions, lovingly reading off-camera lines for other actors. Even more than that, I see Abdul as a modern-day philosopher king (he'll get me for that.) Really, the man has *been* there! He is a veritable treasure trove of wisdom and knowledge on history, current affairs, and just about anything else. As an actor, he is again one of those extraordinary talents like Bruce Page [who] make a director look good by being brilliant at every turn. My life is truly enriched by Abdul's presence in it."

I can't say that I had a personal friendship with all of the wonderful actors in this movie, but I did find a good friend in Abdul. He visited my home, we went out to some restaurants together, and I caught him in a truly wonderful stage appearance.

Abdul is easy to get to know. He's one of those really special people who open up to others quickly and invite them into their world without reservation. He also happens to have spent a lifetime on the stage, and I just *love* "theatre people," having been one of them since I was twelve. My fondest memory of Abdul, outside of his sparkling character work in this movie, is his breathtaking performance in *Ma Rainey's Black Bottom* at the OSF in Ashland the summer of 2005. This is a consummate actor who can reach right into your insides, tear out your heart, put it up in your throat, and then return it to its proper place beating just a bit faster . . . without you ever knowing how he did it. That is, he doesn't seem to be acting at all. He gave the same kind of performance as Chef. *Bravo* my friend!

About *CWG*, Abdul says, "When you make your first film, you're full of passion and [you] can't wait to put your talent out there to be seen. Then it sometimes becomes a job and you show up for the check. *CWG* restored my passion for film acting.

"It was good to be on a set where the passion for a project was running through everyone. To have my passion for my work restored, to feel that connection with everyone, reminded me that God is in us all; [it] showed me the things we can accomplish when the expression, the connection, and the passion is there. Thank you for this project. The world needs it."

Jerry McGill (as Oscar)

JERRY McGILL   JERRY McGILL   JERRY McGILL

The character of Oscar was first conceived as a retired Army drill sergeant, hard-nosed man. But, after meeting Jerry McGill and hearing him read scenes from the *CWG* script, Stephen Simon shook his head and admitted that he was going to have to rethink the character.

Jerry is a quadriplegic in a hand-powered wheelchair, but after meeting him you would never think of him as handicapped. The production company called Jerry back to read two more times before Stephen personally called him on the phone to tell him that he got the part.

One of the most special moments I have ever experienced at a casting was the moment just after Jerry left the audition room following his reading for the role of the campsite manager, Oscar. This was one of those times I described earlier. The place was absolutely still. The room was in shock. No one said a word. Finally, this from Stephen, looking at me in disbelief: "Well, there goes every idea I came in here with about the camp manager!"

The reason this moment was special is because Jerry had no reason to believe that he was right for this role—and every reason to believe that he was not. Like it or not, casting is done at the first level by type. If a person is just way "out of type" for a particular role, he or she is rarely considered.

Jerry pushed through all of that. And, to Stephen's credit, when Jerry maneuvered himself into the room in his wheelchair our producer/director opened his mind and just let the possibilities flow. The result was a magical moment that I don't think any of us will ever forget. The actual manager of the campground was neither black, nor a paraplegic. Stephen didn't care. "This guy is a really good actor," he said. "And he's won the role."

That's what I like about Stephen as a director. He's open to the unthinkable, like he was when Zillah Glory auditioned. Here was a young lady with zero film experience. It's one thing to get into films in a small supporting role in which you're hardly noticed by anyone except your family. It's another thing to start out in a feature role that has you up front, on camera with the leading man in several strategic and important scenes.

Stephen didn't care how inexperienced Zillah was, and he didn't care how "out of type" Jerry was. He went for it, and cast each of them. I stood on the sidelines and watched all of this at the auditions and just whistled in soft amazement. The outcome: bravura performances both.

About Jerry, Stephen says, "I think there's a John Lennon line much to the effect of 'life is what happens to you while you're busy making other plans.' Jerry could not have been more ill-suited to playing the role of Oscar the way the character had been written in the script. When Jerry came into the room I had no idea how to even respond, but I did notice a change in the air density all around us. Something special was afoot. Jerry read the character and just blew us all out of the room. He has an amazing and quiet dignity mixed with a wonderful sense of humor! (The "maid" line regarding the bathrooms in the park was created by Jerry.) Every time we discussed other actors to play the role, we just kept coming back to Jerry. It quickly became apparent that we had to change our whole concept of the role. This was one of the most magical moments of the film, let alone the casting process. Jerry stepped in and just owned the part of Oscar."

Jerry proved his worth as an actor and his endurance as a man in take after take, hour after hour, in the harsh cold environs of the outdoor homeless park set. Everyone who witnessed Jerry's performance saw that he nailed it!

Jerry McGill became the youngest member of the National Theatre Workshop of the Handicapped at age sixteen when he starred as Tiny Tim in a benefit performance of *A Christmas Carol* opposite a young Christopher Reeve. At the 52nd Street Project, another Manhattan theatre company, Jerry performed as their first actor with a disability. As an actor, writer, and filmmaker, Jerry is at the forefront of a movement to feature more people with disabilities in performance media.

Renee Prince: Production Designer

Renee Prince came to head the art department of *CWG* from a very unique background. Renee began her career life with a graduate science degree doing research with dolphins. She came to believe that dolphins lived the Golden Rule and that their ultimate message was love. "When you are in the water with dolphins," she said, "they fill you up with joy." Renee became disillusioned with science when, while working with the U.S. Navy, she saw the loving nature of the dolphins perverted. When dolphins began to go crazy and die, she quit the project in protest.

Renee was thirty years old when she discovered that her ability to think three-dimensionally had artistic applications in drawing, painting, and sculpture. Eventually she began art direction work in the Portland film community. After the dolphin experience, however, Renee felt like she had had a "falling out with God." In working on *CWG*, she found a synchronicity that had personal meaning for her. When she talked to Stephen late in the crew assembly process, an opening suddenly occurred, and she was asked to head the department and recruit the seven others required to fill the needs of art direction, props, and set decoration.

"With Stephen," she says, "your potential is somehow realized."

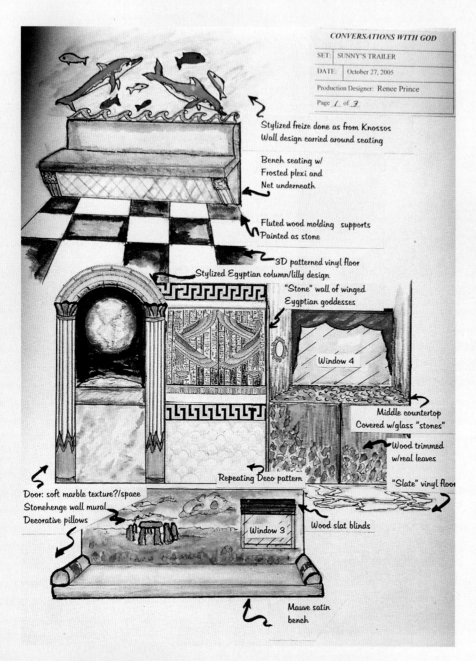

Stylized freize done as from Knossos
Wall design carried around seating

Bench seating w/
Frosted plexi and
Net underneath

Fluted wood molding supports
Painted as stone

3D patterned vinyl floor
Stylized Egyptian column/lilly design

"Stone" wall of winged
Eygptian goddesses

Window 4

Middle countertop
Covered w/glass "stones"

Wood trimmed
w/real leaves

Repeating Deco pattern

"Slate" vinyl floor

Door: soft marble texture?/space
Stonehenge wall mural
Decorative pillows

Window 3

Wood slat blinds

Mauve satin
bench

Renee's color rendering of the interior details of Sunny's trailer

I'm going to share something that I know Renee will kill me for revealing. This woman was very, very ill just prior to and during a part of the shooting of this movie. Still, lying on her bed she decided that she was going to see the project through. She knew that at that late date she could not be easily replaced, and that "the show must go on." She jumped in there and "made it happen," and very few people will ever know what it took for her to do that—the strength and the commitment and the fortitude. That's the word. Just good, old fashioned *fortitude.*

Of course, she's a wonderfully artistic person with enormous talent. But now I know that she's also an exceptional person who understood that, really, it was about more than just allowing the "show to go on." Renee has been deeply touched by *Conversations with God* in her life. It brought her back to God. And she was determined not to let anything stand in the way of her doing everything that she could do, through her art form and her work, to help get the message of the book out. As it was for many others, work on this film was for Renee not simply a job, it was a mission.

Neale's Livingroom / Kitchen Set with Dressing

Renee's color rendering of Neale's living room with set dressing

"Renee is one of the unsung heroes of the film," Stephen says. "To get the look of the film as rich and detailed as it is, with the budget that she had, is a miracle right up there with the 1969 Mets! More than that, Renee is a tireless and devoted creative artist who gives every ounce of her soul every minute of the day. I am blessed to have been able to bring her in and I don't know what I would have done without her."

Renee has been a lead scenic artist and a sculptor for special effects on diverse projects such as *The Abyss, Alan Quartermain and the Lost City of Gold, Army of Darkness, The Fabulous Baker Boys,* and *Nightmare on Elm Street V.* She has demonstrated an ability to use any artistic medium in satisfying the film director's scenic needs and thus has moved into the ranks of feature film production designers.

Laney D'Aquino: Art Direction

LANEY D'AQUINO   LANEY D'AQUINO   LANEY D'AQUINO

Laney D'Aquino as art director is often seen with prop master Austin Van Campen on the run between the sets and their stash of items to solve any visual idiosyncrasy that may pop up in a movie frame. Laney first concerns herself with the emotional content of the scene, and then with the camera position, before she spot checks all elements of the set design during rehearsals. Solving visual problems is her job, and she never wants her department to hold up production. And how does one achieve the insight to see with such a detailed, critical eye?

"By working on it," Laney says. "By thinking about how film scenes look, and how they are framed . . . for years and years."

"Laney was the person on the set [who] Joao and I could always turn to in the moment with an outrageous request for a piece of art direction—and Laney would always have it at her fingertips," says Stephen. "In addition to what she did during production, Laney was also our storyboard artist in pre-production. She sat in a room with Joao, Jeff Bates (our visual effects supervisor), and me for almost a hundred hours while we designed every shot in the film on a blackboard. Laney would patiently watch the way we were designing the shots and then go away and draw each frame of the film for us. For a director and a director of photography, planning is everything, particularly on a film where you have twenty-five days to accomplish a vision of the film that could have easily taken thirty or forty days instead. To truly keep to a schedule, you really need to compile a detailed shot list for every scene before you even start shooting on day one. Laney took those shot lists and brought them to life in the most extraordinary storyboards I have ever seen. And, she did it all with her trademark smile intact. Laney is one of the most positive people I have ever met, and that demeanor sure served us well as we spent those one hundred hours in a small room together!"

Muriel Stockdale: Costume Designer

MURIEL STOCKDALE   MURIEL STOCKDALE   MURIEL STOCKDALE

Muriel Stockdale is an example of the varied talents being drawn to the spiritual cinema community of filmmaking activists. She is director/founder of ISE-NY, a spiritual cinema community whose creation was an offshoot of Stephen's spiritual cinema tour. ISE-NY brought Stephen to New York in June 2005 for its first film festival, which consisted of four days of discussions, workshops, and networking opportunities for "a collective of practical and artistic people from all corners of entertainment, film, theatre, media, communication, and innovative arts dedicated to envisioning and creating empowering, positive, and spiritually nourishing entertainment."

Muriel brings more than twenty-six years of costume design experience to the project. Her creative efforts have been seen on film, television, and the stage in programs for Disney, NBC, CBS, PBS, ABC, and others. She was also a long-time faculty member in the graduate design department at New York University's Tisch School of the Arts.

In her next project, *New York City Spirit*, Muriel directs a feature-length documentary that celebrates the spiritual diversity of a major city. In a screening for the *CWG* cast and crew prior to the first day of principal photography, her preview of *New York City Spirit* was met with cheers.

Stephen says about Muriel: "Muriel's job was an incredibly tricky one. She had to design the clothing in the film in such a way that everyone would think it was natural clothing, not the work of a designer. She accomplished that brilliantly. Take a look at Fitch and Chef on the one hand, and characters like Leora and Carly on the other hand, and you see a great artist at work. Muriel is also one of the people I met on my journeys to establish spiritual cinema as its own genre, and her passion for the work itself is present in every fiber of her being. She was truly one of our "go-to" goddesses, not just for her brilliant creative work, but also for her love and support."

Working on *CWG* was a demanding job because of the pace and the weather. When needed, thermal underwear, rain gear, gloves, and hand warmers had to be ready. Photos of every costume variation had to be kept for continuity. Martha Hines, costume supervisor, was always on set with an eye for wardrobe details. Angela Hill, costumer, and the wardrobe production assistants completed the team.

For Muriel, the wardrobe trailer is an "alchemical oven" that transforms the actors as the people serving them are transformed. She recognizes that creating pure transformational entertainment is a huge responsibility to

Costume concept for the character Fitch

the film's ultimate audience, and that everyone involved must hold the center of pure intention in this new paradigm of moviemaking.

Muriel designed for the character of Neale a completely natural look in blues and grays to enhance actor Henry's striking blue eyes. Muriel saw Sunny as a mystical goddess. She dressed actress Ingrid, then, in flowing and layered contemporary lines within a red and orange color palette.

On a very busy day when the tasks seemed overwhelming, Ingrid gave Muriel a polished heart-shaped rock. Viki

Costume concept for the character Sunny

Martha Hines, the on-set monitor of all things wardrobe

also gave her a rock—a plain rough one—and said to her, "Now you can complete it." Muriel puzzled over the question of how. Then she compared the two small stones and realized that Viki's rock appeared to be the unpolished part of Ingrid's heart-shaped one. The encouraging message came through—with clear intention, manifesting completeness can be easy and can come in a surprising way. This aphorism is as appropriate to a costume designer as it is to a spiritual filmmaker. "Polish a life that seems plain and incomplete."

Dennis Connors: Line Producer

DENNIS CONNORS   DENNIS CONNORS   DENNIS CONNORS

The entire cast and crew took humorous note when line producer Dennis Connors was drafted into the bit part of the jackhammer operator who upsets Neale as he is waiting for a job interview callback near an outdoor public telephone. The fact that Dennis' company is named Jackhammer Films made for perfect casting.

Dennis' story is like that of many creative people on this film who made a conscious choice to leave the centers of the entertainment industry for a lifestyle more suited to a focus on the family. During his career in Los Angeles, Dennis' production company was a major player in creating brand name commercials all over the world. However, the frenzied lifestyle ultimately became intolerable. Now, twelve years down the path, Dennis is living in Ashland and happy that he made the move. His Jackhammer Films there has provided executive production management for CWG.

In a film where the creative producer, Stephen Simon, is also the director, having Dennis on set and in the office to handle the production load was important. Dennis solved the on-set contingencies so that Stephen could stay focused on working with the actors, camera department, and his assistant directors.

"There was no way that we could have done this film without a strong and knowledge-able line producer like Dennis," says Stephen. "Managing the day-to-day operational details of a film and directing it at the same time is impossible, so I leaned heavily on Dennis, and Gary Kout, our production manager and associate producer. The fact that the film came in right on schedule and budget is a testament to Dennis' ability to manage dozens of logistical issues at once. Dennis is also a very upbeat and warm man, so the crew always knew he was looking out for them. And I will always be grateful to Dennis for protecting a passion he and I share. Somehow he found a way to help us figure out how to schedule Mondays in such a way that we were always home to watch the second half of Monday Night Football!!

Gary Kout: Unit Production Manager

GARY KOUT GARY KOUT GARY KOUT

On *CWG*, the roles of the line producer and the unit production manager often merge, but Gary Kout as the unit production manager is the chief administrative officer of the film and its budgetary controller. "Gary's job is always to say *no* when we ask for more money," Dennis says.

"The production team always has to have one guy who worries about each dollar and where it is being spent. Gary worried about every *penny*—and [this] is one of the main reasons we came in on budget and schedule," says Stephen.

Gary describes the organization of a film company in terms of a wagon wheel. The outer rim represents the director's world, where all crafts and talents come together. The many spokes of the wheel represent the individual departments that often do not communicate directly with each other. At the center, or hub, of the operation is the production office that coordinates the whole. Gary, like Dennis, has impressive credentials in the production of commercials, music videos, and feature and documentary films.

In 1996, Gary took a break from filmmaking and led a 14,000-mile, four-month motorcycle trip from Los Angeles to the southern tip of Argentina to raise money and awareness for the American Cancer Society and Save the Children. In 2001, he rode in the Canada-U.S. AIDS Vaccine Bicycle Ride. Then, in 2003 Gary moved his family from Los Angeles to Ashland so his two daughters could grow up in a healthy, small town environment. And like Dennis, Gary is bringing his production experience and his artistic sensibilities to spiritual cinema projects. Both men demonstrate a passion for life, and they both prove that life and work are not mutually exclusive: witness the growing vibrant film community in Southern Oregon.

A cacophony of voices vibrates from an adobe-colored office building off E. Main Street in Ashland. Everyone is engaged, from producer to intern. Every computer is popping e-mails. Every space and chair is occupied. A hundred decisions are being made every hour. Money is being exchanged. Promises are being made. Disappointments are occurring. Phones are ringing off the hook. Management skills are making it possible for this team of filmmakers to keep so many balls in the air that professional jugglers would quake at the numbers, feeling that at some moment the balls would fall and assume the rolling posture of chaos.

A camera truck has broken down en route from California, been repaired, and resumed its journey at midnight. Someone in production is calling the driver every half-hour to gauge his progress. By late afternoon, however, it is clear that scheduled camera tests will have to be postponed. Meanwhile, accommodations and incredibly intricate travel schedules are still being arranged for cast and crew; locations are secured, props leased, shooting schedules published, and storyboards amended. There are wardrobe fittings and closed rehearsals with the director and principal actors. There is an editorial conference involving the director, the film editor, the visual effects supervisor, and the director of photography. The base camp managers are meeting, too. In every department the drumbeat increases and the players move to its incessant rhythm. It is the Wednesday before the first day of principal photography that begins at 5:30 AM the next Monday.

A psychoanalytical study noted that a human being could manage associative relationships with about 230 individuals. A genius might manage 260 or even 280. After those numbers, recall of names and intents are lost. Considering this scientific fact, what occurs in the production office of a feature film the week prior to cameras rolling should be impossible. The completion of any feature film is a miracle of human collaboration.

When you have educated yourself in film production and have the ability to multitask twelve hours a day, you can become a production coordinator like Dawnn Pavlonnis and her assistant Elle Martini. Both are married women with ambitions to produce and direct.

Gary Kout on set with production coordinator Dawnn Pavlonnis

Elle Martini, assistant production coordinator on set

Between the two of them, they have worked on more than one hundred films, television productions, commercials, and music videos.

During production, Dawnn and Elle are the lifeblood of the infrastructure of the film. A film crew of seventy people requires constant attention, monitoring, scheduling, and coordination. As Stephen said, "Dawnn and Elle are the best production coordinators that I have encountered in my thirty years in the business. I never had to worry about anything [not] being where it was supposed to be, and every crew member loved them both."

Medford

Bruce and Henry Czerny as Neale confer with
Stephen on the first day of shooting

Medford, at the center of the Rogue Valley in Southern Oregon, hosted the start of principal photography of *CWG* on Monday, November 7, 2005. The vacated former Carnegie Library building downtown was transformed into a Portland Employment Office, where Movie Neale, wearing a neck brace, is desperately seeking work. Exterior filming began in a cold rain that turned to sleet as Neale arrives at the building. Inside the Carnegie building basement, sets were constructed for the employment office and other office environments dictated by the script. The character, Bob Friedman, the original publisher of *Conversations with God* and played by Joe Ivy, was introduced in a scene shot here as well.

While extras huddled around propane heaters on the empty first floor between scenes that first day, actress Greta Oglesby rehearsed her part as an unemployment counselor with Henry for the scene they would shoot later. When Greta had filled out the audition form months earlier, the character had no other name than Heavy Set Woman, and that is what she

Actor Bruce Page as Fitch

wrote. Casting screeners, however, read her writing as "heaven sent woman" and gave her special attention. Greta is a cast member of the OSF and an award-winning performer in dramas and musicals, so perhaps "heaven sent" was the correct reading after all.

The next day, another Medford location stood in for Neale's Portland apartment. In the scene, Neale and his landlord are in conflict on the fifth floor of a low-rent apartment building. Neale is burning his unpaid bills in a trashcan when the landlord arrives to deliver a past-due rent ultimatum. The sun shining through the apartment window is generated by an 18,000-watt movie light mounted on the platform of a 126-foot high Condor crane.

Joe Ivy in his first scene as publisher Bob Friedman

Stephen Simon on the first day of shooting with Kent Romney of the Sound Department

Outside the apartment living room, one-half the width of the narrow hallway is occupied by camera monitors and sound equipment. Director of photography, Joao Fernandes, sits on an apple box in front of the camera monitor while Stephen Simon kneels on the floor, watching the scene play out. In the dark, crowded hallway a figure appears offering a tray of cut broccoli and cherry tomatoes around a plate of dip. It is Rachel Lipsey, the angel of Craft Services, who has come up the elevator with this refreshing snack. Joao munches broccoli between giving headset instructions to his camera operator. It is mid-afternoon on a day that began for the crew at 4:30AM. Later, in a scene shot down the block from the apartment building in a street entry office, a chiropractor tells Movie Neale that the car crash he suffered actually broke his neck.

November 7, 2005 was a tough day for me. It was almost a year to the day since my very first serious conversation with Stephen about making this movie. I wanted to be *on the set*, part of the action, when the filming began. But I'd promised Stephen and Henry that I would stay away to give Henry the space to create and "get into" his character. So, on this morning I sat in my home in Ashland, musing over what I was missing. I was just twenty minutes away from the shoot, but I might as well have been in New Zealand. (Come to think of it, I *love* New Zealand, and on that morning it would have been better to be there!)

I'd been invited by Stephen to drop by the shoot location to share coffee and donuts with the technicians at Crew Call, but I knew that if I went down there turning around and leaving as the actors arrived and shooting began would be just about impossible. So I stayed away altogether.

When we first talked in November 2004 about this movie being made, I had imagined myself walking around the set every day, chatting with the cast, kibitzing with the director, joking with crew . . .

Director of Photography Joao Fernandez in action on the first day

Neale gets the eviction notice from his landlord

David Kelly as the human resources counselor

I never thought about the stay-out-of-the-way-of-the-actor angle. I should have, of course. As I said before, I've had enough stage experience to realize that it just couldn't work with me hanging around all day, every day. I just never put it together in those terms. And then the first day of the shoot arrived. By that time I *had* put it together, our agreement was in place, and I was feeling totally non-invested in the outcome.

In retrospect, I see that this is exactly what I needed to be; not only to provide the actor playing the role of Neale plenty of room to maneuver, but also to keep Real Neale from going stir crazy on the set, having ideas pop into my head right and left, wanting to make creative suggestions here and there, seeing things that I might imagine should be different, and bleeding from the mouth from biting my tongue hour after hour as the shoot continued.

Henry as Neale burns his past-due bills

The time for trust had arrived. I had to turn everything over to Divine Order. I had to release and let go. I had to trust God; I had to trust our producer/director (who, on the set of a film, IS God); and I had to trust the process called filmmaking, in which many of the people on that set, from Stephen and Joao and Henry on down, had been fruitfully engaged for many years.

So I sat at home that morning and endeavored to think of something else, which is like trying to ignore an elephant in the living room. Fortunately on that day, and on many days during the shoot thereafter, I got calls from my pals in the company—sometimes from Viki King, sometimes from videographer Ed Keller, sometimes from others— keeping me up to date. Stephen himself phoned several times in the early evening just before turning in

Henry and Stephen confer

(he was going to bed as soon as he could those days, having to be on the set before dawn most mornings). He would tell me how fabulous the dailies were, and that things were going even better than he could have hoped for.

So for me at this point it was about trust, trust, and more trust.

Artificial sunlight by crane

Stephen directs Henry and Gretta Oglesby in the unemployment office scene

Stephen and crew watch the monitors during first day interiors

Stephanie Angel: Script Supervisor

STEPHANIE ANGEL   STEPHANIE ANGEL   STEPHANIE ANGEL

Stephanie Angel got her first script supervisor credit as an assistant on *The Bridge of San Luis Rey* (2003), which was shot in Spain and starred Robert De Niro, Kathy Bates, Harvey Keitel, and F. Murray Abraham. She was still a college senior doing a project for her self-designed degree in Film Expression & Spiritual Thought. By 2004, Stephanie was writing screenplays and directing short films and music videos. Before coming to *CWG*, this prodigious young woman already had script supervisor credits on six feature films.

The script supervisor is the director's and the film editor's best source for the continuity of a film. Her notations, cued by the director on his take preferences for each scene, are the detailed record of progress on the filming. Stephanie must note every character movement, every piece of clothing, every set detail, each departure from script, and every nuance of a scene as she views it in her personal monitor. No one on the set knows the progress of the film better than the script supervisor. It is the perfect chair, albeit a demanding one, to learn the craft of filmmaking. Stephanie Angel is also an active member of ISE-NY. She met Stephen on his original 2002 *The Force Is with You* book tour.

Stephanie wears a trick-of-the-trade glove to prevent repetitive motion stress

"When I started looking for a script supervisor, the search began and ended with Stephanie," said Stephen. "Having met her on my journeys, I got to know her as both a person and as an extremely talented filmmaker. I'm going to enjoy watching all the films Stephanie directs in the future."

Stacy Michaelson: Extras Coordinator

STACY MICHAELSON   STACY MICHAELSON   STACY MICHAELSON

Stacy Michaelson was the on-set extras coordinator and production assistant. Like Jackson Rowe, one of the film's two associate producers, her senior high school project was to work on *Indigo*. With the promise of a job on *CWG*, Stacy took a semester off from college to work on the film.

It's fun being an extra in a movie. Ever been one? I appeared as an extra in *The Exorcist* many years ago. Isn't that an ironic twist? They were filming some scenes at a home in the Georgetown neighborhood of Washington, D.C., and I went down from my home in nearby Annapolis, Maryland to see if I could find my way into a crowd scene. I did. I also appeared in what is called a silent bit in one or two other films being shot in Baltimore and Washington. Too, I was a bit player in *The Seduction of Joe Tynan* starring Alan Alda. Being a bit player means that you actually get to mumble something on camera. I had to join the actor's union to be able to do that.

When they began filming *CWG*, I thought, well, at least I can go down to the set and be an extra in one of the crowd scenes. Nope. No dice. Stephen said, "Neale, you are too recognizable to your readers. Do you think they don't know what you look like? And if they saw you in the background in one of the shots, it would pull them right out of the movie. I can't have that happen. You can't be in the picture. Sorry."

"Not even as a walk-across?"

"Not even as a fuzzed-out face in a crowd of a thousand people."

"That's too bad," I told him, "because I'm really good at being a fuzzed-out face."

Then the mischief began.

I was telling some of the members of the company about my being banned from the film when

Extra with fire barrel at Emigrant Lake set

impish Ed Keller said, "Oh, c'mon. We can *sneak you in.* We'll slip you on to the set as part of the crew. We'll give you a cap and some sunglasses and a scarf around your face [it was really cold some of those mornings in December, so they could actually have gotten away with this!], and no one will know who the heck you are. Then we'll sneak you into the background just as they're about to shoot. C'mon, it'll be fun."

I really wanted to do it! I wanted to pull a Hitchcock and appear in my own film! And mostly, I wanted to prove to Stephen that not only would no *Conversations with God* readers notice me in the shot, but even *he* would not see me there!

In the end I chickened out.

What if he *did* spot me in the crowd? I could see it now: They've taken all morning to prepare for this shot. The set is finally ready, the lights have been tweaked perfectly, the make-up artist has had last looks, the actors are in place, and the director has called "Action!" The scene is going magnificently, the actors are nailing it, the technicians are stunned by the magnificence of the performance . . . then, from out of nowhere comes the director's voice. He shouts, "Cut, cut, CUT! *Damn it, Neale, get OUT OF THE SHOT.*"

Everyone freezes. All eyes are on me. The actors are boiling, and the crew members are shaking their heads, and the company accountant is off on the side punching buttons on a calculator, and then Stephen is walking over to me with a gun in his hand . . .

So I decided not to do it.

"Cluck, cluck, cluck," Ed Keller said to the chicken the next time he saw me.

Scott Cervine (as the Landlord)

Scott Cervine had an international career as a stage magician. For some of his illusions he employed the Pagganini theme so familiar from Stephen Simon's *Somewhere in Time*. Scott credits Viki King's book *How to Write a Movie in 21 Days – The Inner Movie Method* with igniting his passion to make films as an actor, writer, director, and producer.

Scott joined the 2005 Spiritual Cinema Festival-at-Sea where his touted film *Out of Proportion* was screened. The film was then selected for the August 2005 The Spiritual Cinema Circle DVD. On the cruise Scott also met casting director Kathy Wilson, who later cast him on *CWG*. Citing Stephen Simon as his inspiration for making movies that matter, Scott edited the feature film *The Life Coach*, produced *Closer Than Ever* for submission to The Spiritual Cinema Circle, and—at the time of his *CWG* role—was in pre-production of *Dying to Meet You*, a feature film about a past-life love triangle.

"Scott is one of the multi-talented filmmaker/actors that we are so proud to be nurturing and supporting through the Circle," says Stephen. "His humor and humanity shine through every project he takes on."

Karen Fitzgerald (as Chiropractor)

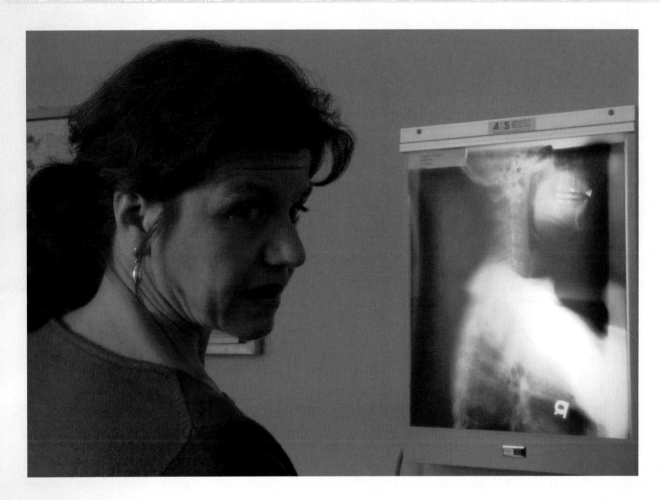

Karen read the *Conversations with God* series five years prior to auditioning for the movie. At first, she says, she resisted the premise of the book: that she could have a personal relationship with the prime energy of Creation. Then she made a breakthrough. Karen came to The Spiritual Cinema Circle on a link from Wayne Dyer's website, became a member, and then joined ISE-NY. During ISE-NY's film festival in 2005, she attended Stephen's intensive workshop on how to get spiritual cinema projects produced. Here Stephen held impromptu readings from one of the first versions of the *CWG* screenplay. Karen performed a dramatic reading of a scene, which moved all of the workshop participants. Later she traveled to

Neale is told by the chiropractor that he has a broken neck

Ashland to audition for the movie and won the role of the chiropractor who tells Neale that he has broken his neck.

Karen came to acting after the age of thirty, and since that time she has performed dozens of leading roles in regionally produced musicals and dramas, in addition to appearing in commercial advertising. Her appearance in *CWG* was facilitated by her fierce determination.

Crystal Dawne (as Chiropractor Assistant)

CRYSTAL DAWNE   CRYSTAL DAWNE   CRYSTAL DAWNE

Crystal Dawne read all of the books in the *Conversations with God* series. Getting her mail in Los Angeles one afternoon, a copy of *Vision Magazine* fell open to the announcement of the open casting call for *CWG* in Ashland. She was determined to audition and land a role in the movie. To save money, Crystal stayed in a youth hostel on her arrival in Ashland. Her determination was to be the first person in the casting call line, so she appeared at the Ashland Springs Hotel at 4:30 AM on the appointed day. The hotel night clerk hardly knew what to do with her. At 6 AM a second person, also hoping to be the first in line, found Crystal at the entry door. Both young women had their hearts set on playing the role of Carly. Crystal did not get the feature role, but her enthusiasm and ability landed her the role of the chiropractor's assistant.

"There was no way that Crystal wasn't getting a role in *CWG*. Show up at 4:30 AM? THAT is dedication! Even though she was wonderful in the role, her scene didn't make its way into the final cut of the film; however, she did participate, and it was wonderful having her with us," says Stephen.

Crystal is a furniture designer, a children's TV series writer, and a working actress, writer, and documentary film producer originally from Manitoba, Canada.

Bus Scenes

Stephen and Zillah prior to the bus scenes

Medford also served for various street locations in scenes with Carly, played by Zillah Glory. Neale and Carly have a playfully provocative relationship as workday passengers on the same city buses. Although Carly is in her twenties and Neale in his forties, Neale has come to rely on Carly for her bright energy and wit. "When I'm with you, things just seem to fit," he tells her. "I like myself when I'm with you. Like you're my best friend. I know that you feel that, too, right?"

In character, Neale and Carly at the bus stop bench

Well, no. Carly doesn't feel that way at all, and she deflects Neale's intentions in no uncertain terms. The brief appearance of Carly in the movie

Henry and Zillah mug through bus windows

Rachel Lipsey works the craft services snack table outside her converted school bus while her father, Steve, visits the set

is played for both humor and pathos. When Zillah Glory as Carly reacts to Neale's declaration of attachment on the bus stop bench, cast and crew realized that she was perfectly cast.

Henry as Neale with his stand-in Dayvin Turchiano

Vic Simon: Winning Extra

VIC SIMON   VIC SIMON   VIC SIMON

Vic Simon, a pilot captain for American Airlines, has a passion for movies. As a member of The Spiritual Cinema Circle, he entered its contest to name the winners in fourteen major categories of the 2005 Academy Awards. The grand prize was an all-expenses paid trip to be an extra in the filming of *CWG*. Vic, no relation to Stephen, got the news at his home in Dallas, Texas within fifteen minutes after the Oscar telecast. He was the sole entrant who had picked all fourteen winners. Vic can be seen in a bus scene with Henry and Zillah showing off his wristwatch.

Medford Airport

Bob and Neale negotiate with Sharon and her Putnam assistant, played by Michael Traina

The real Bob Friedman, publisher at Hampton Roads Publishing Company, was well known to Stephen and Neale because he had published their books. Both were present when actor Joe Ivy came into the room to audition for the role of their friend Bob. Joe Ivy walked up to them and spoke a few words, and then the two men looked at each other in disbelief. Stephen says, "Joe Ivy was more Bob than Bob!"

As an actor working in Los Angeles and Portland, Joe Ivy knew locations manager Randi Brahm and casting director Kathy Wilson, both of whom steered him to the *CWG* audition. Joe had moved near Ashland, where his wife worked at the Shakespeare Festival.

Joe's big scene was filmed in the Jackson County Airport in Medford on Day 17 of the shooting schedule. Bob and Neale have come to the airport to meet with Sharon Parker, a savvy New York City publisher played with verve by Carolyn Hennesy. Sharon has brought a million dollar offer to the table to acquire worldwide publishing rights to *Conversations with God, Book One*. Neale almost comes out of his seat when Bob refuses the offer in the dramatic negotiation scene. They walk away, and then Sharon stops them with a counter offer, but the deal cannot be made until Sharon answers Neale's question: "Why do you want to publish this book?" In a softening of her professional façade, Sharon gives the non-commercial answer that Neale needed to hear. "I think your book can change the world."

It took an entire day that began with a 5:30 AM crew call to film the three airport scenes. Moving inside for the first full day of interior filming, cast and crew looked entirely different without their knit hats, rain hoods, and heavy coats. Women crew members who might have been bald under their winter hats suddenly appeared luxurious in long hair. Everyone remarked on the wonderment of indoor toilets after what seemed like a month of cold outdoor portalets.

Wherever the film company goes, Continental Catering, with chefs Larry Larson and Jimmy Leming, must follow with their mobile kitchen and dining tents. They began serving hot breakfasts before dawn to the crew of the equipment trucks. At the lunch break, Bern Case, director of the airport, and the security team that had facilitated the use of the facility as a movie set, sat down with the *CWG* cast and crew. Director Case happily reported that he and his staffers were actually enjoying the experience, although they were surprised by the

Stephen reviews shot notes with script supervisor Stephanie Angel

size of the film company and the amount of equipment and concentrated activity that was involved in making a movie.

Carolyn Hennesy as Sharon Parker comes from a moviemaking family. She remembers growing up on dark studio sets that she associates with the presence of free donuts. Her aunt is the well-known actress Barbara Rush. Carolyn read and underlined *Conversations with God, Book One*. She reports seeing the character of Sharon Parker as someone who represents an intellectual approach to the power of the book.

"Carolyn came in to audition for another role in the film," Stephen remembers. "She did a very good reading for that character, but I knew she was Sharon Parker from the minute she walked in the door. When she had finished reading, I wanted to gently broach the subject with her, but she took one look at me and said, 'Okay, Stephen, you want me to play the Sharon Parker role, right?' Busted! 'Yes, absolutely,' I replied. 'And you know you fit that role perfectly.' 'Of course I do, but that's a one-day role, and I want to be in Ashland and on this movie a lot more than that!' Well, she got the one-day role, was absolutely magnificent playing it, and we had a lot of fun that day in the airport."

Before leaving the airport, Movie Neale has an encounter with a waitress

Joe Ivy as publisher Bob Friedman

who mentions that she is a single parent one semester away from earning a college degree. When leaving the tip, Neale considers his good fortune and then empties his wallet—a whopping $100 gratuity.

If Zoe McLellan as the waitress looks familiar, perhaps you remember her from a supporting role on forty-nine episodes of the TV drama series *JAG* or from *Dungeons & Dragons, The Movie* (2000). She has also appeared on *Star Trek Voyager*, *The Invisible Man*, *Silk Stalkings*, and *Diagnosis Murder* on TV, and in eight feature films. Another interesting synchronistic aspect and example of how Stephen gathers the tribe is that Zoe had attended one of Stephen's workshops some years before the making of *CWG*.

The scene dramatized here needed no "dramatization" at all. It was, just as it actually happened, one of the most dramatic moments that anyone could have in their life. The real contract talks on *Conversations with God* took place at the airport in Atlanta, Georgia, where I was catching a connecting flight while on a book tour. The between-flights meeting was held

Zoe McLellan get "final looks" as the airport waitress

in a conference room, but Stephen decided that a small room with no windows and a single oval table was not visually interesting, so he placed the meeting in the airport restaurant.

Of course, I will not forget that meeting as long as I live. Bob Friedman, the co-founder and president of Hampton Roads Publishing Company, who first put *Conversations with God* into print as a soft cover book (and who, by the way, published *this* book), was introducing me to the president of Putnam, who had expressed an interest in acquiring *Conversations with God* and reissuing it as a major hardcover fall release. Bob said she wanted to meet me to see if I was "the real thing."

"In other words, she wants to make sure I'm not some kind of weirdo flake who made this whole thing up," I said to Bob.

"That's right," he replied.

"Great. Terrific. No pressure."

"Neale," Bob soothed. "Just act normal."

"I thought you said she wants to make sure I'm *not* a weirdo flake," I chuckled.

The film dialogue of our exchange was lifted pretty much from real life. Eric questioned me about what happened, who said what, etc., and managed to capture the moment almost word for word.

The short scene with the waitress at the end of this sequence is a little bit of an embarrassment to me—but I wasn't successful in lobbying it out of the movie. It got into the film to begin with because I told a little anecdote about my personal life in one of our scripting meetings. It was Viki King, I believe, who asked me how it felt after living in a tent at a camp-ground to get a huge publishing contract from Putnam, and I told a very personal story of how I over-tipped a hard-working single-mom waitress a couple of days later out of sheer exuberance. In real life this moment occurred in a restaurant in Ashland two days after that airport meeting on the East Coast. In the first draft of Eric's script this was a stand-alone scene. When he moved the contract negotiation scene to the restaurant, Stephen lit up. "Hey, this is perfect!" he said. "Now we can cut the separate waitress scene and just make it the end of this run." Everyone agreed that the new placement made for a tighter story. I voted for cutting the scene altogether.

"Oh, man," I said to Viki. "If you guys put that incident into the movie, people are going to think that as soon as I got a little money, I started throwing it around. What a gauche per-son!"

"Neale," Viki said, "it's a very human moment. What we can show here is how elated you were, how in touch you were with your feelings and with your good fortune—and that your first impulse was to share it. That says something about you. Besides, we're not making this up. This actually happened."

"Yeah, but putting that in the movie . . . I don't know. It seems so self-serving."

"So when has that stopped you before?" Stephen grinned. "Relax," he added. "We'll put it in the making of the movie book that you never tip more than eighty-five percent."

Henry as Book Neale in glasses

Bookstore Challenge

BOOKSTORE CHALLENGE   BOOKSTORE CHALLENGE   BOOKSTORE CHALLENGE

One of the challenges of telling the *Conversations with God* story is how to convey the wisdom and insights of the book without simply reading from its pages. Screenwriter Eric DeLaBarre has dealt with this issue in a series of flash forwards that shows Neale after the publication of the book as he responds to bookstore and lecture hall audiences.

In a dramatic sequence filmed at the Barnes & Noble bookstore in Medford, Neale is responding to questions from a gathering of thirty-two readers when he is interrupted by a distraught mother who has lost her eighteen-year-old adopted son under painful, overwhelming circumstances. Georgia, dressed like a woman who has lost concern for her appearance, charges down the book aisle to assail Neale's view of God. She accuses God of vengeance, and she demands to know from Neale how his God is capable of allowing such a terrible loss to befall her family.

As Neale appears in venues around the world today such encounters are not uncommon, but every one of them begs the question of how Neale can respond to such impossible questions. The encounter with Georgia is based on an actual moment when Neale had to somehow reach into the spiritual center of himself and speak the healing truth that the individual most needed to hear. To be in attendance for those moments is electrifying because intellectually, we realize that the mind cannot possibly conceive an appropriate, much less a deeply healing, response.

The role of Georgia is played by Ruth de Sosa, a veteran actor with great personal warmth. Ruth was conscious that every performance in *CWG* must serve the high goal of the film. In take after take—from master shot, to close-ups,

Henry and Ruth hug while standing on a height-leveling platform

to crowd reactions—Ruth delivered an emotional intensity punctuated with palpable pain that made her character so real, so present, that crew and extras wept time and time again. On the first two takes, Stephen himself emerged from the blackout monitor tent with tears in his eyes, and he draped his arm around Ruth as they walked the aisles of the bookstore, readying for the next take. When the scene was completed, Stephen led the applause by cast and crew for Ruth's remarkable performance.

Stephen says, "The role of Georgia is one of the most challenging emotional roles in the film. Playing that kind of emotion on stage is one thing. You do it once a night and that's it. On film, you need to repeat the performance several times from several different angles. I made sure we were completely ready to capture the first take perfectly because that kind of emotion often is best captured right out of the gate, so to speak, and Ruth was letter-perfect. Not just on take one, either. Ruth hit every emotional beat every time. It's an amazing moment of vulnerability, and she is brilliant in the role."

As for Henry as Neale, the truth of the moment in his own lines, and moreover, in his silent reactions to the grieving mother, required no less intensity than Ruth's. Henry must make us believe that Neale is capable of falling out of his limited vision of his own being into that place of the divine heart where all answers are available, even answers to impossible questions. That Henry was able to perform that wonderful, quiet moment of release also produced tears of joy.

The end of the Barnes & Noble shooting day required an exterior setup as Neale and Leora leave the store and talk about the remarkable encounter with Georgia. In the darkness of early evening a heavy, wet snow had begun to fall as the cast and crew emerged. Excitedly, Stephen and Joao made quick adjustments to their shot lists. Joao raced off to commandeer the crane and camera crew, and Stephen ran to talk to Henry and Vilma. "When it snows, you have to capture all your footage—and all your coverage from each angle—before it stops snowing," Stephen states. "If it stops snowing at the wrong moment, your camera angles won't match, and you have to start all over again. We were truly blessed that night. We got absolutely everything we needed, and it stopped snowing right after I said 'Cut' on the last take. Casting by God, weather by Goddess!"

Ruth de Sosa begins her dramatic scene

Neale signs his book for a customer as Leora, played by Vilma Silva, watches.

I believe that God speaks to all of us, all the time. As *Conversations with God* says, it's not a question of to whom does God talk, but of who listens. The exchange dramatized in the bookstore scene played by Henry and Ruth actually occurred in real life. It was one of those occasions when I listened very carefully to the Voice Within, and God gave me—and the lady confronting me—the answer for which we both were looking.

It was also a turning point for me because it was a moment in which I realized that I could love others unselfishly and openly. I had been carrying a message that my mother had given

Errin "Moose" Connors, third electric crew, gets a surprise birthday cake during lunch in the Barnes & Noble parking lot.

me when I was a small boy and she had sat down, at my request, to do a palm reading for me. (I'd watched her do them for all the neighbors and half the family, and I begged her to "read my palms, read my palms!") She said that my palm lines showed that I would never love anybody. Now I know that Mom never meant to hurt me, but that stuck with me all of my life, and frequently the memory of that moment and that message came back to me.

Stephen, Eric, Viki, and Joao listened very intently when I told them this story, as well as the incident many years later involving the lady who had read my books and had so emotionally challenged me about God.

Stephen comforts Ruth after an emotional take

Once more, Eric captured almost the exact words of my encounter with the woman. Once again, only the location of the incident was changed, and again for production purposes only. The intimate scene that follows, in which Neale visits his mother's grave, is true to life. I actually did that, and I remember seeing tears in the eyes of Stephen, Eric, and Viki when I told them about all of this. They all got me back. Tears filled my eyes when I saw these two scenes in the film's first rough cut.

The crane crew prepares for a shot in a heavy, wet snow outside the Barnes & Noble parking lot.

Land Mind Studios Sound Stage

LAND MIND STUDIOS LAND MIND STUDIOS LAND MIND STUDIOS

Land Mine Studios in Medford is a converted cold storage warehouse where Rogue County pears were once processed and shipped. The four-story processing areas comprising 40,000 square feet are now devoted to film and video departments. The gigantic sound stage, with its forty-foot ceiling, was the former pear-shipping warehouse. For *CWG*, the art department built and the set-dressing department furnished Neale's house with its living room, kitchen, and bedroom. The last week of principal photography was produced here.

The camera setups for Neale's process of hearing God and beginning to record his conversations with God on yellow legal pads were complex. On Wednesday, December 7th, there were twenty-five setups, and twenty-eight on the following day. Some of these setups required a camera crane above the living room and moveable walls to get the appropriate angle or to facilitate a dolly shot with the camera platform on tracks. The passage of time over the seasons necessitated constant redressing of the set and a fireplace that was lit or dark according to the script. Green screens were placed outside all of the windows so that the visual effects wizards could later project onto them various season changes.

Stephen had promised relief from the cold, wet Oregon December weather, but that did not mean that the working pace of cast and crew was lessened. The "cast" for this final week consisted mostly of Henry, whom the entire company had come to admire for his professional ability, endurance, and good nature.

The scenes where Neale questions God—and gets answers—are very crucial to making the movie work as both a dramatic entertainment and as a spiritually rewarding experience. Recreating and sustaining Neale's epiphany over time on the screen required enormous concentration and a heightened sensitivity among crew members, who had to realign the camera and lights and redress the set for season changes, as Henry (as Neale) had to maintain a focused continuity in his dialogue with the unseen source of the Divine while constantly

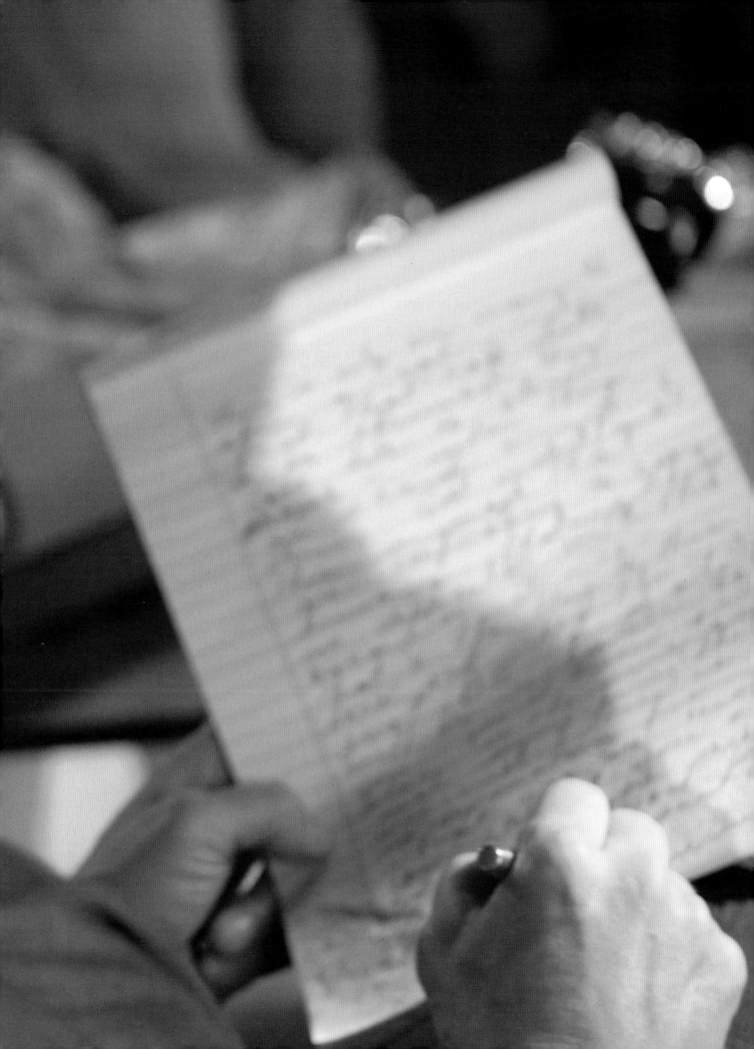

undergoing wardrobe changes. Stephen required quiet on the set throughout this critical process that lasted three days. In these scenes, months are condensed into movie minutes that capture the essence of Neale's profound experience. Everyone involved was conscious of the responsibility of being faithful to this re-enactment. In honoring these creative moments faith was not only being kept with Neale, but also with the audiences who would respond to these scenes from their own spiritual perspective.

The audience is further served in responding to the revelations voiced by Leora, as played by Vilma Silva. Leora, the friend who types the book manuscript from Neale's handwritten pages, is the first person to understand its message and to have her life altered as a result.

"I don't want to spend my life making a living, Neale," she says with passion. "I want to spend my life making a life. A life that makes a difference. A life that is built on love and compassion."

There is no sequence in this movie that was discussed more in the

months before production than the God Talks to Neale scenes shot on the sound stage in Medford. That's understandable, of course. The movie is, after all, called *Conversations with God*. In the end it is about the precious moments in these scenes. It is not about anything else. All else simply leads up to them and leads away from them. Those moments are the fulcrum.

In the scripting conferences Stephen, Viki, Joao, and Eric went over these scenes from every angle. Mostly I sat and watched, though I did tell them in detail what the experience was like for me. It wasn't difficult to remember those details; this is not an experience about which one's memory is likely to be hazy.

I told Stephen that I was deeply concerned about this depiction from the very first scripting conferences in January 2005. "Me, too, pal," he said quietly. "Me, too."

We knew we were walking on the edge here. What actually happened to me was other-worldly in the sense that nothing in this world can explain it. The trick was to put it on film in such a way that it was not *too* other-worldly for an audience to accept—yet not so padded down that it became uninteresting . . . to say nothing of being untrue.

Key set production assistant Dan Jesperson makes notes

Over and over again, at different times and in different places, Stephen would say to me, "Tell me again exactly how it happened." I knew that he was trying to get a clear picture of just what the experience was like, and then to get the picture again and again so that he wouldn't lose it.

I kept telling him that I heard a voice—as clearly as any voice I have ever heard in my life—that felt like it was *outside of me*, speaking to me from over my right shoulder. Then, the voice seemed to move inside. I have likened it to a "voiceless voice," something like the sound of one's own thoughts.

Of course, you can't put a voiceless voice on a soundtrack. So there you have it. I left it to Stephen to create this sequence of my taking "dictation" from God, which took place over many months and through several seasons in the way that he thought would work best cinematically. Then I got out of the way.

I want to tell you, this was not easy. As I mentioned before, standing aside from this part of the creative process took every ounce of patience and trust that I could muster. I stayed away from the set when the shooting of this sequence was taking place, too. Not *easy*, my friend. *Not easy*. This scene was about the most important moment in my life and I couldn't even watch it being shot, much less offer suggestions.

Phew.

When I saw the sequence in the rough cut, I finally relaxed. "Yes," I said. "That's exactly the way it was . . . like someone was talking to me, like I was taking dictation . . . like I was having . . . well, a *conversation*.

I was like a mad man, getting up in the middle of the night, every night, picking up the pen and . . . asking questions, getting answers, and writing, writing, writing until I had yellow legal pads everywhere, filled with this . . . this *dialogue*. Every night I was awakened at the

Neale and Leora rehearse as first assistant director Jesse Nye makes adjustments

same time—between 4:20 and 4:30—after which I couldn't sleep, so I just gave in and gave up and picked up the pad and pen and started in again. Stephen found a way to capture the essence of that experience. Eric found a way to write it. Joao found a way to photograph it. Henry found a way to act it out.

It is the longest single sequence in the movie. It covers the better part of a year in a few minutes. It brings the messages of *Conversations with God* not just to Neale, in the scene on the screen, but to everybody in the audience as well.

From book to movie! *We made it!* This is what we'd set out to do in my home a year earlier, this is what we dreamt of on that day in November 2004 when we first agreed to undertake this project and, by golly, *we made it*.

Neale to the Set

Out of consideration for Henry who was playing him, Neale did not appear on the live movie set until the next-to-last day of principal photography. On that day, Stephen took Neale on a walk through the sound stage house set and then into a production office where he showed Neale the opening first few minutes of the film. Although the private moment between the two dear friends was behind closed doors, their emotions upon leaving the office were apparent. Back on the sound stage Neale, Stephen, and Henry briefly posed for photographs together, and then Neale was gone—less than an hour after his arrival.

My visit to the sound stage was for me very emotional. I had to get in and get out of there fast. Shooting on the film was nearly complete. Stephen knew that I wanted to see at least one scene being shot. He called me at home.

"Hey, bro, why don't you come down to the stage tomorrow and watch us do the shots leading up to you getting the call from the publisher . . ."

"You sure I won't bother Henry?"

"He's done all the important scenes now. This is an easy scene. He doesn't have to go deep for this. Be a good day for you to come. And you should really see the apartment they built for you before they tear it down."

So I went over and ducked in and out. I saw the terrific interior set the company had constructed. I watched Henry film a short sequence (the one where he writes on the back of Hampton Roads' first rejection letter for my manuscript, "Read any ten pages! I dare you!"). I witnessed Joao performing his magic up close. And when the company took a break, Stephen and I shared an emotional moment in the production office near the sound stage. "I want you to see the first three minutes of the film. We just got the assembly."

After this viewing, misty-eyed, we went back to the stage area and had some quick pictures taken with Henry. I shook hands with some of the crew, and then slipped out.

"Thank you, God," I said as I drove home. "Thank you, God. Please use this movie as you used the books—to get the message out that You're talking to all of us, all the time; that what happened to me can happen—is *happening*—to everyone."

That line is right out of Eric's script. My gosh, Eric, now I'm quoting *you*.

Emigrant Lake

Stephen and first assistant director Jesse Nye work in the dark shadows as the dawn high-lights the crests of the mountains and the lake glows like electric slate where the flutter of geese wings ripple the silence and presage their determined honking. The coming of day is timeless, like the unfolding of the human struggle, and as if to reinforce the epic moment, a wind blows up to accent the bitter cold. When the first shots of the early morning are com-pleted, Stephen thanks the company and applauds them with gloved hands. Suddenly, all around him, frozen faces crack into smiles.

Stephen wanted torturous weather to emphasize the plight of the homeless men, and if nature would not provide rain on cue, a 3,000-gallon tanker truck with fire-width hoses and treetop metal sprinklers would suffice for a drenching. Much tedious labor, including the extension of a 126-foot crane with a light platform, was needed for the nighttime downpour

Book Neale returns to the camping park to discover it sold and abandoned

scene where Neale struggles to erect his tent. Many "dry" rehearsals were done to limit necessary wet ones, but everybody realized that the two actors and the camera crew were going
to get soaked on a cold night where chills went to the bone.

The catering crew arrived at 3:30 AM to make the coffee and ready the breakfast foods,
including eggs to order, for the cast and crew of seventy. The crew began at 4:30 AM, and cast
members began arriving at Emigrant Lake shortly after 5:00 AM.

Base camp is alive with the hum of generators. The only lights come from the headlights
of entering vehicles and the doors and windows of the trailers parked in rows. Beyond the
scattered equipment trucks, grips move with flashlights. Further away from the lights, one can
look up to see a star-filled sky in the clear, cold pre-dawn. There are necessary conversations

here and there by people unrecognizable in the dark, and on a curb outside the wardrobe trailer two young women are distressing new boots with a food grater, sandpaper, and rasps to make them appear the apparel of a homeless man, shoe size 14.

The original campground where Neale came to destitution as a homeless person was too near the noise of a major highway to be suitable for a film location so Emigrant Lake, five miles east of Ashland, was substituted. The park covers 1,467 acres including more than twelve miles of lake frontage. Emigrant Creek and later Emigrant Lake were named for the emigrants who once crossed the Cascade Ranges over the southern route and then came down the stream into the Rogue River Valley.

Flocks of migrating Canadian geese honked overhead during the November days of shooting there. The 5:30 AM crew calls and camera setups were begun in darkness on mornings when Craft Service was issuing chemical foot and hand warmers to everyone. The dawns were spec-

The movie crew makes rain as Neale approaches the campground

tacular as the sun rose above the mountain peaks across the lake from the homeless campsite set. The book cover photo of Henry as Neale was shot on such a morning, and the film crew marveled to see racing shells making training runs across the frigid surface of the lake.

Base camp, with its equipment trucks, wardrobe and makeup trailers, catering kitchen on wheels, and principal actor trailers was in a large paved parking area adjacent to one of the park's major picnic shelters. The homeless campground was erected on a lake point some one hundred yards away from the sound of the electrical generators.

The art department headed by production designer Renee Prince, art director Laney D'Aquino, and set decorator Travis Zariwny created a homeless camping set that amazed both cast and crew. The authenticity and detail of it was worthy of a display in a natural history museum. No one believed that their team of prop masters and set dressers erected the large outdoor set and dressed it in two days.

Strike the Set

Neale accepts a souvenir cup from the set as Viki King observes.

On the day that the homeless camp set was to be struck, Neale requested an opportunity to walk through it with Viki King. Those who were there for the dismantling, and for later photographs with Neale, stood out of sight as Neale carefully surveyed the scene. He even took down the tent that had represented his first shelter there. Later, he threw out some of the contents of the small cabin that stood for his second accommodation.

At the Chef character's shelter, Neale picked up a spoon. The artifact was like the penny in Stephen Simon's film *Somewhere in Time* that takes the character immediately back to a past life. It was clearly evident from Neale's emotions that the memory of those tormented days had struck him. Later, in a very generous gesture to actor Bruce Page, who was off the day Neale visited the set, Neale talked to him emotionally about the homeless men he had met in the original campground. He told Bruce that his character Fitch in the movie was drawn from several personalities. The people around the two men stood back in awareness that a very powerful moment was occurring.

Neale sits on a stump at the lake, looking back at the homeless camp set.

Neale has an emotional moment as he holds a spoon from Chef's kitchen.

I've already talked about my very precious moments with Bruce Page on the campsite set the day we tore it down. Actually, it was my idea to be there and help strike it. I heard a report that shooting at the location had been completed, so I called Stephen and asked him about that.

"Any more shots to get at the campsite?"

"No, we're wrapped out there."

"Oh, great, because I really want to go out and see that location. I want to see that set, walk on that set."

"Well, you'd better hurry," Stephen said. "They're striking tomorrow."

"Hey!" I chirped. "How 'bout if I go out and *help them!* I would like to actually tear down that set *with* them."

"Great idea!" Stephen allowed. And so out to the location I drove the next morning, arriving just as the crew was getting ready to strike.

Everything got very quiet when I walked onto the set. Most of the crew members knew who I was. Those who didn't were told in whispers, "This is the guy who had the experience they made this movie about." So people just quietly stopped what they were doing and let me slowly move around the set . . . remembering . . . thinking . . . of how it was when it was *not* a movie set, but real life.

The moment wasn't lost on me. My mind was reeling. You know how fast time flies. And here it was, just a few years after the actual experience, and I was walking around a campsite made to look totally realistic down to the last detail. Philosophical thoughts raced through my head: "Which is the movie? That, or this?"

Actor Bruce Page talks to Neale about his portrayal of a homeless man.

Jesse Nye: First Assistant Director

JESSE NYE   JESSE NYE   JESSE NYE

Jesse Nye got his first professional view of feature filmmaking as a production assistant on *The Horse Whisperer* (1998) and *The Thomas Crown Affair* (1999). His assistant director credits began in 1998 with the TV series *Sex and the City*, followed by *Law & Order: Special Victims Unit* and *Third Watch*. On feature films, Jesse worked on *Gangs of New York* (2002) and *Basic* (2003), among others.

"The first assistant director [AD] on any film is, along with the director of photography, the director's most important ally during production," says Stephen. "The first AD is responsible for making sure that each day's shooting progresses in a timely fashion, that each shot includes all the elements that the director has designed, and that the set is run quietly and efficiently. The first AD runs the set and coordinates with each department as each shot is set up and executed. A first AD has to know everybody else's job on the set as well they know it themselves. In addition, a first AD is the director's right arm and left eye, collaborating on the ever-changing landscape of a shooting day. Good first ADs are hard to find; great ones are as rare as white buffaloes. Jesse is a great one, and even that may be underestimating him. He was always the first guy

to the set and the last [guy] to leave. He knew the shot list backwards and forwards, and he had an incredibly intuitive sense of where the heart of each scene was for me. He was constantly at my side, alternatively encouraging and cajoling me, always positive and utterly indefatigable. Every Sunday morning we would meet for breakfast and work out the following week's plans. I guess the best way I can summarize Jesse's contribution is by saying that I will never make another movie without him at my side. Never!"

Set Decoration

A homeless shelter as constructed

Set decorator Travis Zariwny got two days to tech-scout the film's locations and make sketches of his immediate concepts relative to the screenplay on a 5" x 7" drawing pad. Without twelve years of production design and art direction experience, including eight years as the art director of the filmmakers' laboratory at the Sundance Film Festival, he could not have fulfilled his assignment.

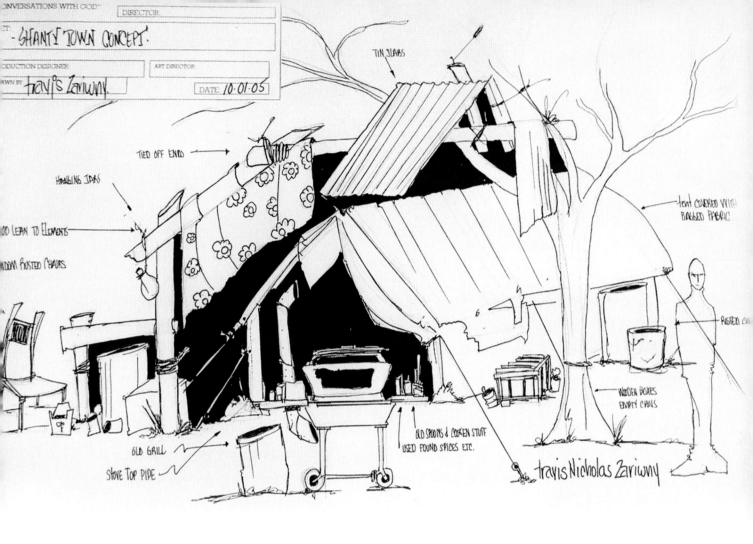

The shanty town homeless park as first drawn

Travis holds a degree in political science, but he has also trained as a movie camera operator and held the key position as a focus puller on feature film camera crews. He also writes screenplays and has aspirations to direct. These multiple skills and higher movie ambitions do not make him unusual in this film company.

The Homeless Camp

THE HOMELESS CAMP THE HOMELESS CAMP THE HOMELESS CAMP

The homeless camp where Neale sets up his small tent in a driving rain seems like a place of last resort; and yet, even there, with life reduced to survival instincts, there is friendship and even compassion among those who appear as social outcasts. Here Neale learns the camp rules from Oscar, as played by Jerry McGill, from his wheelchair. Here Neale encounters Fitch, an alcoholic who haunts Neale's sense of reality, and Chef, who shares a meal of potluck goulash from his hobolike shelter. And here, too, Neale is assaulted by Oakley, played by OSF actor James Peck, for poaching a trashcan where aluminum cans may be salvaged for a five-cent redemption. Survival in the homeless camp is that marginal; and yet, when Neale has the opportunity for a job interview and an escape from extreme poverty, Fitch and Chef come up with money for bus fare to town and a hearty breakfast. They see for Neale what they cannot see for themselves, and they are willing to make personal sacrifices in the name of hope.

As meaningful as these relationships are with his fellow homeless men, it is Sunny, the

Rain stands provide a hard rain on Neale and crew for shots around the tent.

The picnic grounds site for the homeless camp is restored to its pre-filming condition.

mystical resident of the camp, who provides the transcendent courage for Neale to end his downward spiral. Admitted to the inner sanctum of Sunny's trailer, where no homeless camper had gone before, Neale is counseled for his return to life by the beautiful, enigmatically wise woman. Later, when a restored Neale returns to the campground and trailer park to reconnect with Fitch, Chef, and Sunny, he finds them all gone and the property sold.

Floodlights on a crane above the trees light the camp for the nighttime rain scenes.

135

Oakley attacks Neale over possession of aluminum cans

Alyson Bradshaw applies a "final look" to Henry as Ingrid watches

*Later, when Neale gets a job, he upgrades to a tiny campground cabin
where he can entertain his two friends with a pizza party*

Jerry McGill as Oscar explains the camp rules to Neale

James Peck as Oakley naps beside his cache of redeemable cans

Neale, Chef, and Fitch dine on "Mexican Goulash"

Daisy, the Set Dog

Daisy gets elevated by production assistant Levi Anderson so she can see what's happening on the set.

The first morning at the base camp on Emigrant Lake a Jack Russell Terrier appeared without a collar, and she appeared with an appetite. Robert Platt, the five-ton-camera truck driver, fed the sweet little dog and kept her warm in his truck cab. He named her Daisy, and although Robert tried to find her owner, all efforts through animal welfare agencies failed. Daisy became well-known and well-petted by the entire cast and crew. As the film locations shifted, Daisy rode with Robert, who had already made the commitment to adopt her.

Jackson Rowe: Associate Producer

JACKSON ROWE   JACKSON ROWE   JACKSON ROWE

Jackson Rowe grew up in a family where both his father and mother were professional actors. His father Doug, who acted with Jackson in *Our Town*, says that his son can act, too; and, indeed, Jackson has a small cameo as a checkout counter employee in *CWG*. Doug is an accomplished actor, having appeared in countless movies, television shows, and plays—including a memorable run as Willy Lohman in the OSF production of *Death of a Salesman*. Doug even has a memorable scene in *CWG* as Harry, a janitor who encounters Neale at a television station. Not to be left out, Doug's wife and Jackson's mother, Catherine, plays a mysterious woman who is always seen with a little boy across a table from her.

Jackson, or Jack, always wanted to produce films. One day he went to the home of a high school friend and saw movie posters on the living room wall. The girl's father was Stephen Simon, and Jack wanted desperately to talk with him. Stephen, who had himself been mentored by legendary producer Ray Stark, immediately took on the mentor role in Jackson's life. In Jack's last year in high school, his senior project was to work on Stephen's film *Indigo*. With *CWG* in pre-production, Jack decided to skip film school for a job as Stephen's personal assistant. Because Stephen included Jack in every stage of the film's development, Jack received a movie education par excellence and was quickly elevated to the role of associate producer, quite a feat for a twenty-year-old!

"Jackson is an amazingly talented and dedicated young man," says Stephen. "I've never met anyone who is as in love with producing movies as Jackson—except maybe me at his age! He learned everything so quickly on *Indigo*, was so incredibly insightful during our script development and pre-production on *CWG*, and was so involved in every aspect of production, that he earned his associate producer stripes. He and I drove to the set and home together every day, and I came more and more to rely on his perspective. He is going to be a hugely successful producer in his own right very soon. I just hope he'll remember me if I ever need a job!"

Viki King says about Jack, "Jackson is hitting on all cylinders in every area of his life. Watch for Jackson. He will one day be going up for his Oscar as a producer."

Another of Jackson's secondary roles on the *CWG* movie set was working with Ed Keller as producer of the *Behind the Seen* documentary and monthly video diaries for The Spiritual Cinema Circle.

Mystery Lady

She was ubiquitous on the set as she stood in a long shag coat watching every camera take, silent, and unlisted on the call sheet of daily film activity. The lady with the silver hair and the concentrated look on her face—who was she? She was Dawn Elizabeth Rae, a master's degree candidate in Conscious Evolution at The Graduate Institute of Milford, Connecticut. She was researching her graduate thesis on mentoring and very carefully observing her subject— Stephen Simon.

Sunny's Trailer

Ingrid Boulting as Sunny prepares for her scene in a quiet place

In the shooting script, Scene 71 between Neale and Sunny in her magical candle-lit trailer is a moment highly anticipated by cast and crew. The emotion of it, the tenderness, and the vulnerability affected everyone who worked on it inside and outside of the trailer.

Viki King observed in talking about Scene 71 that, "Everyone participating had climbed a mountain to be in the film. They had showed up in the reality of divine order and its synchronicity with a willingness to step up and up and up into what spiritual cinema can be. The film is just pretend, but the filmmakers are real people who respond to the process of being together for a creative purpose. The greatest gifts that we give to each other are compassion, cooperation, and loving support.

"Can you imagine," Viki asked, "finding your way out of a homeless campground to publication fame, and now a movie being made about that transition? Neale can look at it now and realize that he could not have lived any other way in order to arrive at these moments in time."

Neale is moved by the generosity of Fitch and Chef

Neale's homeless friends provide cash for
bus fare and breakfast

Neale wears the clean shirt that Sunny has ironed

Neale begs for jackhammer relief

To get a job interview return call, Neale has to stake out the only phone he has access to—a roadside public one. Unfortunately, a road repair crew appears and the sound of a jackhammer threatens to spoil the illusion that Neale is not homeless. Neale begs cooperation to no avail. Amazingly, the jackhammer generator fails momentarily just as the phone rings, and Neale has a window of opportunity to make his interview appointment.

There then comes the day when Neale has saved enough money to leave his tiny cabin in the park for a small rental house in town. Fitch, his homeless friend, accompanies Neale to the bus stop. And, although the two men have endured much over the previous months, there is the self-evident prospect that they will never see each other again.

The bus used to take Neale out of the park in the movie is a decommissioned local bus purchased at auction by Scott Eason, a former bus company driver. Scott recalled that this specific bus was in service in 1991–1992 and on the same route that Neale had to travel to get to work, and was thus almost certainly one of the very buses that Neale had taken during the real events depicted in the movie.

When I first arrived in the rain at that campground, I thought I might never get out of there. I was 49 years old, walking around with a broken neck, completely unemployable, scrounging around in dumpsters and garbage cans for pop bottles and beverage cans so that I could turn them in at the convenience store for the five-cent deposit. You can't imagine how desolate that was, how empty I felt. I felt my life had ended. It was over. There was nothing else to live for. I was utterly convinced that I would never get out of there. I understand why guys turn to drink. Nobody has to explain that one to me. Nor does anyone have to explain to me how tough it is, once

you're on the street, to get yourself out of there, to find a job and get going again. Just getting anyone to *look* at you, much less hire you, can be the major achievement of the day.

I will never forget how I felt when I got a weekend job at a Medford radio station, moved off the grass and into a cabin at the camp, and then—finally—out of the campground altogether. I never thought I'd do it. I don't know how I did it. It was a wonderful confluence of events. A radio station looking for a man to do the only job I could do! A classified ad *telling* me about that job that I just happened to glance down and look at in some soggy newspaper! A campground phone booth where the noise was deafening—until the very second I needed it to be quiet!

"No one would believe this story if I told it to them," I said one day during those January scripting conferences.

Line producer Dennis Connors as Mr. Jackhammer

"Well, they'd better," Stephen responded, "because we *are* going to tell it to them."

"But I know what you mean, Neale," Eric allowed. "Your story is so improbable at so many junctures and in so many ways, it *is* unbelievable. And we only have enough time in this film to tell the half of it. We can only write so many scenes."

"Will the scene where I leave the campground be one of them?"

"Are you kidding?" Eric erupted. "That's *got* to be in. There's a *huge* message in that for anyone who's ever felt like throwing up their arms and saying, 'What's the use?' No, no, Neale. That's *got* to be in."

So . . . if *you* have ever felt like that—if you are feeling a little like that right *now*—get the DVD of this movie and take a look at that scene again, the scene where I am leaving the park. I want you to know and I want you to understand, Yogi Berra was right: *The game ain't over 'til it's over.*

Just when you think it's the end, it's the beginning.

Remember that. Always remember that.

Neale says goodbye to Fitch

Ashland, Oregon

ASHLAND, OREGON   ASHLAND, OREGON   ASHLAND, OREGON

When Neale came to Ashland, Oregon he unknowingly joined the ranks of many pioneers before him. The initial settlers had followed the gold rush to the Rogue River Valley, where they established a tent camp in 1852 on the banks of a little stream at the foot of the heavily forested Siskiyou Mountains. Soon a town emerged with a sawmill, a flourmill, and a general merchandise store to service the mining traffic.

Ashland then discovered another bountiful resource besides timber: mineral water from Lithia Springs. The soda and sulfur waters became famous as a cure-all that could be drunk or used for bathing. By 1914, Ashland was a spa town and Lithia Spring waters were piped to the park, railroad station, library, plaza, and several hotels.

Where there are spas, there are audiences for cultural entertainments, and in 1935 the town built an Elizabethan stage and presented its first Shakespeare play. Today the Oregon Shakespeare Festival, a Tony Award-winning production company, presents eleven plays in rotating repertory from February through October in three distinctive theatres. With so many excellent actors and directors in town, three additional theatres producing alternatives to Shakespeare opened. Ashland also stages an Independent Film Festival each April that showcases eighty feature films, documentaries, and short films in a five-day movie fest.

The beautiful mountain landscape, four-season climate, and the cultural sophistication of Ashland have attracted the restaurants, bookstores, art galleries, and shops that you might expect. Many noted authors and entertainment and industry executives have chosen Ashland as their home.

Although the snow doesn't stay long on the streets of Ashland, Mount Ashland—eighteen miles away—is a ski area that receives an average of 300 inches of snow annually on its 23 trails. For summertime adventures, visitors and locals take on wild and scenic whitewater trips on the Rogue, Klamath, and North Umpqua Rivers.

In the 1990s, however, the advantages of Ashland's 140 years of progress were lost on a homeless, emotionally and financially destitute Neale. If he were a pioneer, he would have to become a spiritual pioneer, because all other doors seemed slammed in his face.

Many of the movie locations in and around Ashland are the actual places where Neale experienced his ordeal and where he came to ask for and receive the answers to his life's most challenging questions. Those questions, of course, are also *our* questions—no matter what material status we enjoy. And although Neale now lives comfortably on a hillside above Ashland, he cannot separate himself from the knowledge of what it means to have been humbled. Whatever our social status, what Neale wants most for us is to have our own conversations with God.

In the movie, when Neale first arrives in Ashland he seeks shelter at the home of an ex-wife. Upon arriving there, he just can't bring himself to knock on the door and ask for help, so he ducks into the garage and grabs his old camping gear—a tent and a sleeping bag. Not a moment too soon for as he emerges, it is raining . . .

Neale gets turned away at the back door of a cafe

In the movie, Ashland streets, bookstores, and landmarks serve as background for Neale's odyssey as he seeks employment, experiences social ostracism, and faces the degradation of being caught eating discarded food from a dumpster. Neale is denied the use of a restaurant bathroom because of his shabby appearance, and he suffocates in primal fear in an urban alley as he is reduced to surviving on garbage as a community outcast.

Filming in the heart of Ashland also included scenes of Neale after the success of *Conversations with God* as he hears shoppers praise his book, and later when he signs books in a Main Street bookstore.

Note the subtle reflected brick pattern as Neale and Leora are photographed through a bookstore window

Stephen and Viki confer on Ashland's Main Street

Stephen and crew set up for a scene in a second bookshop

Rejection causes Neale to slump against an alley wall

The Ashland Springs Hotel

THE ASHLAND SPRINGS HOTEL   THE ASHLAND SPRINGS HOTEL   THE ASHLAND SPRINGS HOTEL

Neale exits the Ashland Springs Hotel after applying for a job.

The Ashland Springs Hotel is featured in several *CWG* scenes as Neale applies for a job and works the night shift there. The nine-story hotel was originally built in 1925 and then restored in 1998 as a European-style, seventy-room boutique hotel that is recognized as a historic landmark. Owners Becky and Doug Neuman hosted the open casting call for the movie, and the hotel then served as the six-week home for principal cast and crew members. Stephen was often found conferring with members of the film company in a comfortable living room niche in the two-story lobby. The hotel's mezzanine café and popular Lark's Restaurant became rendezvous spots. Meeting rooms in the hotel were used for initial camera tests and then for many media interviews during the filming.

"When I first moved to Ashland," says Stephen, "I met the Neumans and became aware

Videographer Ed Keller interviews actress Carolyn Hennesy in the hotel's Garden Room.

that Becky had loved *Somewhere in Time* so much that a good deal of the Ashland Springs Hotel redecoration was inspired by The Grand Hotel in *Somewhere in Time*. She nailed it. The ambience of quiet grace and comfort at the Ashland Springs reminds me very much of the Grand, as does the friendliness and courtesy of the whole staff. The Ashland Springs was really our headquarters for casting, rehearsals, and just hanging out. Once you enter that hotel, you never want to leave."

Henry, as Neale, seems happy to have landed the right clerking job.

Final looks. Shashana Kaplan is very aware of the dramatic moment as she touches up Henry's make-up.

Living in a small tent and trying to make it on five-cent aluminum can redemptions, Neale is reduced to seeking leftover meals out of dumpsters. This dramatic sequence, one of the most powerful and poignant moments in the film, was played out behind a Main Street restaurant.

As anyone might guess, this powerful scene—when Movie Neale is scrounging for food in dumpsters—was the most difficult for me to watch. Henry Czerny's acting here is beyond superb. It is clear to me that he was *living* this moment, not merely recreating it. And I was re-living it as I watched him up on the screen. I broke into tears in the back of the theatre at the preview showing during this sequence. It is impossible for me to tell you of the personal devastation that a human being experiences on the day that the consuming of other people's garbage becomes the only way to survive. There is nothing more that I can or need to say about this. It's all up there on the screen.

Neale cries as he eats someone else's leftover burger

Neale climbs out of a dumpster where he has searched for food

Mother and son, played by Lauren Stocks and Carter Haukedahl,
catch Neale eating from the dumpster

For the thirteenth consecutive year, nearly half the town of Ashland—about 10,000 people—line the main street and plaza the Friday after Thanksgiving to see the seventeen-unit Christmas Parade and the downtown buildings come to illumination in a festival of ornamental lights. The film company had positioned no less than five cameras (two on rooftops) to capture this event. Movie Neale is watching the happy families and realizing what he has lost. Sunny is there, too, observing Neale. A gaggle of extras had been gathered and coached on appropriate crowd reactions to Santa and Mrs. Claus counting down the seconds to the dramatic lighting, but otherwise the throng of people on the street went undirected.

At the plaza itself, across the street from the balcony where Santa stands for the countdown, the real Neale Donald Walsch has arrived for a Medford NBC affiliate live interview

Henry dances with Martha Hines of Wardrobe as they wait for the Christmas parade

about the making of his life story into a movie. As the parade neared, a cold drenching rain began, and Neale and the on-camera interviewer are soaked despite the small umbrellas employed.

In an earlier interview for a national television feed, Neale had articulated what he hoped the *Conversations with God* film would accomplish. The movie, he said, could reach people in a different way from his books. In one focused experience, the moviegoer could learn that what occurred in Neale's life could occur in any one's life, and that our lives can change at any moment when we begin a conversation with God—a relationship that is always available.

Neale said that his conversations with God that became a series of books was an experience rather than something that he had conceived. Desperation had put him into the place of appealing to God, and Ashland was where the actual events took place.

Yes, Neale had been that lost man in the Ashland Christmas lighting crowd many years before. Yes, he had felt so distant, so remote from them; but also in that throng of celebrating families, he had resolved to find his way back—back from poverty, back from darkness into light. This very moment was being played out by Henry as Neale, as Neale himself was being interviewed in the plaza. The irony of the juxtaposition was not lost on Neale, or on anyone involved in telling his important story of spiritual restitution.

Here we go with the surreal experiences again. I was very much aware that there were "two Neale's" at the 2005 Christmas Parade in Ashland. Standing in front of a TV camera and being interviewed for the local media was Real Neale dressed in the stylish warm clothes of a person living comfortably while just a few yards away Movie Neale stands in front of a movie camera dressed like a homeless person and shivering in the cold. This juxtaposition had quite an impact on me. I realized that Henry Czerny's "Neale" represented a version of me from *not that long ago*.

I walked around the town plaza in the heart of Ashland where the Festival of Light is centered, and my heart filled with gratitude for the year that 2005 had been. A wonderful *Conversations with God* book, *What God Wants*, had been published in 2005. Another *Conversations with God* book, the last in the dialogue series, titled *Home with God*, had been written and sent to the publisher. A new children's book based on *Conversations with God* teachings, *The Little Soul and the Earth,* had been released. An animated children's television program based on *The Little Soul and the Sun* had been signed and moved into the first stages of creation. A worldwide satellite broadcast,

Ingrid whispers to Henry as they wait.

Stephen directs Henry with Ingrid watching

Extras line the street in chairs to be briefed

global podcast, and Internet radio program revolving around the material in *Conversations with God* had been aired. And *CWG* the movie had been conceived, scripted, cast, rehearsed, and filmed.

Here I was, in the town plaza watching Santa Claus count down the seconds as the crowd held its breath and the whole town prepared for every tree and building to light up. And there, on the other side of the plaza, was this living representation of me from another time. I felt as though I was stepping through a *time warp*. And the greatest gift of all for me that Christmas of 2005 was a realization of what this very unusual moment had brought me: determination and firmness-of-intention can beat the highest odds, life is a glorious opportunity for the creation of our wildest dreams, and we must never take for granted our blessings, but use them to bring the highest benefit possible to others. Lyndon B. Johnson often stated this principle with simple eloquence: "Of those to whom much is given, much is asked."

The Radio Station

The Radio Station The Radio Station The Radio Station

When Neale finally connects with a steady job, he returns to his former occupation as a radio station disc jockey and programmer. He is hired by a frenzied manager named Roy, played by Michael Goorjian, but Neale's most important encounter is with Leora, as played by Vilma Silva. Leora will become Neale's steadfast friend who sees him through the writing, publication, and success of *Conversations with God*. It is Leora who later first reads and responds to the words on the yellow legal pads as she types the original manuscript of *Conversations with God*.

I've spent more than forty years in broadcasting. As I mentioned earlier, I'm doing a new radio program as I write this, carrying the messages of *Conversations with God* to an ever-widening worldwide audience on LIME.com. I'm so grateful for having been given this particular talent. Without it I might never have dragged myself up off the street. Because of it, I was given a second lease on life.

The scene in the radio station fills me with exhilaration every time I watch it because it takes me right back to the moment when I realized that I was not going to have to live outside

Neale begins his relationship with Leora at the radio station.

forever, that I was *not* going to die in that park. This was a miracle for me. I was 50 years old when I hit the skids. If I had been a younger man, I might have been able to shake that off quickly, bounce back faster, to get off the mat immediately. At 50, I wasn't quite so nimble. Mentally, physically, and emotionally I was slower to adjust. And not only was I a half-century old, I also had a broken neck. I felt that all the cards were stacked against me.

Then came the scene you see in the movie, at the radio station. My neck had healed just enough so that I didn't have to wear my brace to the interview. Then there was the gift from some of the guys in the park of half the coins they'd collected that week. And the help of the Lady in the Trailer to get my clothes washed and pressed, my hair shampooed and cut back, and my beard trimmed. These seem like simple things in our day-to-day lives, but when you're where I was *these are miracles.* And when the radio station program director gave me that weekend job on the spot the largest miracle of all had occurred. I was working again! I had an *income.* Not much of one—just $100 a week—but I had an income. (Actually, $100 a week felt like a fortune. And it was. I felt like the most fortunate man in the world.)

Michael Goorjian (as Roy)

Michael Goorjian met Stephen in the mid-1990s when he was shopping a metaphysical love story script. Stephen was the first producer to encourage and support Michael in the spiritual cinema direction. In a continuing relationship, Stephen applauded Goorjian's 2004 film *Illusion* starring Kirk Douglas, which Michael wrote, directed, and co-starred. The film won First Place Feature and the Audience Choice awards at the 2005 Spiritual Cinema Festival-at-Sea. "Michael is an incredibly talented writer, actor, and director and I have believed in him for more than ten years now," Stephen says. "*Illusion* is one of the great films in spiritual cinema in the last several years."

Michael recognizes Stephen as the spearhead of a movement to change the current Hollywood mindset. Although the difference between meaningful films and those that only exploit sentiment is difficult to articulate, Michael believes in the future of spiritual cinema and he looks for every opportunity to work on projects that demonstrate its values.

The one-day role of Roy, the radio manager who hires Neale, may seem trivial to an Emmy Award winner for Best Supporting Actor (CBS-TV movie *David's Mother*, 1994), but Michael now follows his heart in filmmaking. "I'll do any role for Stephen," he says.

Television viewers will recognize Michael from regular guest star roles on the *Growing Pains* series (1985) and as a regular on the ABC hit show *Life Goes On* (1989). He appeared with Nicholas Cage and Elisabeth Shue in *Leaving Las Vegas* (1995) and on the TV series *Party of Five* for four seasons as Justin Thompson. Michael wrote screenplays, co-produced, and starred in feature films leading up to his film *Illusion*.

The Peerless Hotel

The coffeehouse patio where Fitch embarrasses Neale and Leora is part of The Peerless Hotel Restaurant and Bar. The Peerless Hotel is a restored 1900 hotel in Ashland's historic Railroad District that is now on the National Register of Historic Places. Although use of The Peerless might have demanded a hefty fee, owner Crissy Barnett generously allowed her property to be used due to the nature of the filmmaking. "We want to support our film community," she said.

In the movie, just when Neale thinks that he is resuming some sense of normality by reading the newspaper in a coffee shop patio with new radio station friend Leora, who should stumble in but Fitch from the homeless camp. Fitch is drunk and pitifully inappropriate as he offers Neale and his "lady friend" a drink from his bottle. His sexual innuendoes end

awkwardly as Fitch jars the table and spills coffee on Leora. When he tries to apply napkins to her linen slacks, Leora pushes him away and he falls backwards onto the floor. Neale is left to deal with the social upset and to help Fitch back to his lean-to shelter at the homeless park. It then occurs to Neale that Fitch could be the man *he* will become if he stays in the park too long.

Thanksgiving Day

Department heads Sherril Schlesinger (Editing), Lisa Schneiderman (Publicity), and Muriel Stockdale (Wardrobe)

Like many films, many out-of-town cast and crewmembers in CWG could not get home for Thanksgiving Day. Stephen did not abandon them; rather, he invited everyone to The Peerless for a Thanksgiving Dinner feast of Pacific Northwest cuisine prepared by co-executive chefs Stu Stein and Mary Hinds, whose creations have earned a Wine Spectator Award of Excellence. The special fellowship that Stephen hosted with the two of his four daughters who were in Ashland that day included lead actors Henry, Ingrid, and Bruce; consultant Viki King; both assistant directors; department heads including editor Sherril Schlesinger; and gaffers, grips, and production assistants. The fine food and meaningful conversations continued for three hours.

At one table, unit publicist Lisa Schneiderman suggested that each person relate what they were personally grateful for, and in this sharing a spiritual bonding across age and title lines

Actor Bruce Page and casting director Kathy Wilson

was born that all who experienced it will never forget. In all the collective moviemaking experiences represented at each table, no one could recall such a generous fellowship of cast and crew. The awareness that something wonderful was happening made the experience even sweeter.

Although Real Neale had dinner guests at his home, he came down the mountain to The Peerless to congratulate Stephen and the out-of-town cast and crew at the mid-point of the demanding shooting schedule. Neale embraced everyone in the room and visited every table as dessert was served. His appearance was more than a gesture. It was a show of sincere solidarity with those whose dedicated labor over twelve- and fifteen-hour work days were making *CWG*, the movie, a reality.

Still photographer Ben Lipsey, in an unselfish act, left his own Thanksgiving family gathering to capture photos of The Peerless event.

Stephen at the host table with Ingrid and his daughters Cari (standing) and Heather

New Thought Church Scenes

NEW THOUGHT CHURCH SCENES   NEW THOUGHT CHURCH SCENES   NEW THOUGHT CHURCH SCENES

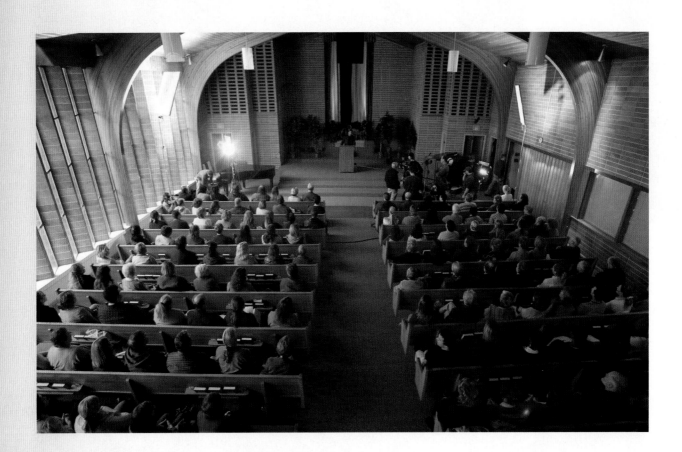

The New Thought Church scenes were shot at the Rogue Valley Unitarian Universalist Fellowship in Ashland. In the movie, this is another of the flash-forward scenes where Neale as a successful author must respond to challenges about his book.

Neale makes the point that there is no separation between financial abundance and spirituality. "Don't you find it odd that we live in a society that devalues our most important jobs? Imagine a world where money was given to those who give us the biggest gifts. Teachers, artists, nurses, policemen, firemen, even writers . . . " A woman from the pews calls out, "and mothers!" and the audience continues their applause and cheers for the neglected occupations.

Suki and Margot Robinson have speaking roles in the 150-member congregation. These

women and three others—Alecia Rice, Suzanne Hodges, and Lisa Platt, who also appear as congregation members—met at The Spiritual Cinema Circle events and bonded with nine other women from around the world. Like many of the four hundred extras who appeared in the lecture hall sequences, these women felt compelled to be present and participate in the movie.

Suki speaks on behalf of feminine energy

The Goddess Circle

THE GODDESS CIRCLE   THE GODDESS CIRCLE   THE GODDESS CIRCLE

From the onset of production, Viki King and Lisa Schneiderman set the space for what came to be known as the Goddess Circle, as Viki brought forth the intention of encoding divine feminine energy into this film. This became the energy that the first-string Goddesses (the dynamic women of the *CWG* cast and crew) held throughout the production.

The first meeting of the Goddess Circle was held on the eve of filming at Viki's cottage, where the women set the intention for the film and for themselves. Together they recognized the powerful effect that the *Conversations with God* books have had in the world and the potential for positive change the film will have. The core of the Goddess Circle met regularly throughout filming to hold the light for the film and its participants.

During the late-night filming at Emigrant Lake, the Goddess Circle reunited for a candle-lighting ceremony. A candle was lit for Stephen and the rest of the *CWG* cast and crew. When the New Thought Church scene wrapped, the Goddess Circle merged with some extras on set near the altar to form a prayer circle. When *CWG* filming wrapped, there was a closing Goddess Circle ceremony. It was another demonstration that what was occurring in and around the filming of *CWG* had many significant dimensions.

The seven goddesses at New Age Ch...
Suzanne Hodges, Alecia Ri...

. to R): Lisa Schneiderman, Lisa Platt,
King, Laurie Farley, and Suki

The Lecture Hall Scenes

THE LECTURE HALL SCENES   THE LECTURE HALL SCENES   THE LECTURE HALL SCENES

The casting call was advertised in the newspapers, on television, and on leaflets in book-stores and shops from Ashland to Medford. Some four hundred extras were needed to be audience members at a lecture given by Movie Neale. There would be dramatic question-and-answer scenes with audience reactions being filmed so the volunteers would be there all day, potentially from 7:00 AM to 5:00 PM. Their reward was a free lunch and a drawing for prizes such as DVD players, gift certificates, autographed books, and crew baseball-style hats.

In rehearsals for the master shot, Stephen interacted with the audience, often humor-ously, on crowd reaction nuances; and before the first take, he told them to "have some fun." More than thirty of the extras were members of The Spiritual Cinema Circle or devoted read-ers of *Conversations with God* who had traveled to Ashland from New York, Pennsylvania,

Stephen addressses the audience extras from the stage.

Ohio, Minnesota, Florida, Alabama, Texas, California, and other states to participate in the filming. In a touching dialogue with audience members during a camera move, three people admitted to Stephen that they had formerly been homeless. After the long first take, Henry as Neale came back on stage to applaud the crowd, and Stephen was right behind him to pronounce them "fantastic!"

At the end of the long shooting day, first assistant director Jesse Nye congratulates Henry as Stephen looks on from the wings.

Gary and Dawn from the production office conduct one of the several prize drawings for the extras.

The crux of this scene, which occurs early in the movie as a flash forward of who Neale will become, addressees some questions that Neale has faced from the public since writing *Conversations with God*. Occasionally, the questioners may seem rude and even hostile.

The first questioner is Daisy, played by Michelle Merring. She is troubled because people don't want to respond to her new spirituality. Neale helps her understand that she must "concentrate on what *you* think of *you*."

Next, a male voice asks if Neale has any regrets about his life before *Conversations with God*. The question has a hard edge, and the audience is uncomfortable. Neale answers, "Many," but the questioner probes, "Care to share a few?" Neale buys a moment with a laugh line, but then centers himself to respond with clear vulnerability:

"I only wish I could have come to this point in my life without hurting so many people, especially those I have loved. But without them, perhaps I might not have come to this point in my life. It is important for all of us to remember that the universe is conspiring in our favor. Always. And in all ways. Despite circumstances and appearances, or our perception of them."

Neale's explanation angers another man in the audience, played by Bill Geisslinger, who stuns the crowd by standing up and shouting, "You've got a lot of nerve!" Neale, too, is momentarily perplexed. The man continues his attack:

"You're a hypocrite, standing up there preaching about God and love. You've been married and divorced a bunch of times. If you talk to God, how come you can't keep a commitment with a woman?" ("When I asked Bill, who is a brilliant, accomplished actor, to play this one-day Angry Man role," Stephen says, "he asked me one of the greatest actor questions I have ever heard: 'If I get *really* angry, can it be three days??'")

The angry man as played by Bill Geisslinger

Neale responds to the angry man in the audience

The tension in the audience is visible as they shift attention from the angry man back to the emotionally stunned Neale. They search his face in expectation as he pauses between the dimensions of his soul. Finally, he answers in an almost weary voice:

"You wouldn't believe how many times I've asked that same question. The women in my life . . . they are all wonderful. And they treated me a whole lot better than I treated them. I betrayed them. I let them down, and my kids, too. I admit that. More than that I cannot say without invading their privacy, and that I am not going to do."

The audience is totally silent, hanging on Neale's naked confession.

"All I can do is love as much as I can from where I am, and try to make every gesture an action sponsored by love."

The angry man, for his own deeply troubled reasons, will not relent. He attacks again, against the murmuring of the crowd. "Sounds to me like you've written a book of lies."

Here, in rude words, is the essential challenge Neale must face from every audience. What qualifies him, a common man, to have a personal conversation with God? *It is the question every spiritual messenger has ever faced throughout human history.*

"If you're asking me did I make all this up . . . the answer is no. But, I will tell you this, I've wondered what you are wondering. Will anyone believe this? Believe me? Will they believe where it came from? I just hope that you make that decision from your own hearts, not from what you think of me personally. And please, don't disqualify or marginalize the message because . . . I am . . . such a fallible messenger."

The audience immediately reacts with applause to Neale's emotional vulnerability while Kay, Sharon DelaBarre, the screenplay author's mother, steps to the microphone to thank Neale for "admitting your mistakes."

"The truth is, Kay . . . I'm still making them to this day. That's why these conversations with God have been such a miracle for me. They came out of my desperate need, my own personal need, to change my life. I'm not sure if I've been successful in doing that the way I'd like, but it is the way that it happened."

The long scene ends with Kay asking Neale, "If God had only one message, his most important message to all of us, and you could put it into one paragraph, what would that be?" Neale stuns the audience with his answer, and then goes off the stage to thunderous applause.

"I can fit it all into five words," he begins as his exit line. *"You've got me all wrong."*

It is 4:15 PM by the time Henry is called upon to redo the scene for the close-ups to a theatre empty except for the audience member actors who ask the questions. Henry has been on the auditorium set since 7:00 AM in hair and makeup (rehearsal began at 8:15 AM.) And yet, after performing the same demanding scene all day, he must somehow give it the same emotional intensity and nuances of humor that he exhibited throughout the day when the live audience applauded his every delivery. A stage actor delivers his lines once a night. A film actor delivers and re-delivers all day long.

Michelle Merring (as Daisy)

MICHELLE MERRING   MICHELLE MERRING   MICHELLE MERRING

Michelle Merring as Daisy is another actress who first met Stephen at a workshop appearance and had been influenced in her personal life by Neale's *Conversations with God.* When she learned that Neale and Stephen were coming together to make the *CWG* film, she scheduled a family vacation with her husband and two small children to Ashland to audition for a role.

Michelle appears as the woman in the lecture hall audience who tells Neale that she finally understands what it means to be awake, but that her friends and family think that her new spirituality makes her seem strange. Neale relieves her concern with humor when he says, "I know exactly what you are going through and the good news is you're not crazy . . . unless we're both crazy, and if that's the case, at least we'll be in good company."

Michelle Merring is a New York native who has performed leading roles in off-Broadway productions and television and stage roles in Los Angeles.

TV Station Interview

Neale meets the TV station janitor, played by Douglas Rowe, who quotes from his copy of Conversations with God

Neale's encounter with a TV station janitor who reads *Conversations with God* and Neale's on-air interview was filmed at RVTV, the Rogue Valley Community cable access channel on the campus of Southern Oregon University. Harry the janitor is played by Douglas Rowe (Jackson's father), who has been a stage actor and director his entire adult life. In 1959, when he joined Equity, he was its one thousandth member, and today he still carries the number 1,000 on his union card. For twenty-five years, Douglas was associated with the Laguna Playhouse, the oldest continuous community theatre in California and where actors Harrison Ford and Mike Farrell got their start. Douglas was also an Oregon Shakespeare Festival cast member for four years.

In the janitor scene, Neale notices that Harry has a sticky-noted copy of *Conversations with God* in his back pocket. Neale's personal attention surprises the man, but Harry then reveals why he reveres the book. "I spent a lifetime in anger towards my father. This book helped me finally, after twenty years of that kind of hate . . . well . . . to forgive my father."

And then Harry admits the even greater lesson. "What I was feeling about my father was really what I was feeling about myself. I had to forgive myself for the feelings I had, the anger I had against my father. I don't think I've ever said that out loud before."

As the camera pans to the interview set, note the two TV producers with clipboards in hand. The dark-haired one is Lisa Schneiderman, the unit publicist, and the taller blonde one is Tara Walsch—Real Neale's daughter. The talk show host is Kimberly Tere, news anchor for KTVL, the CBS affiliate station in Medford. Kimberly covered the *CWG* auditions as a news reporter, interviewed Neale and Stephen, and was asked to audition for the film role. She is a native of San Francisco and a graduate of San Francisco State University.

In the talk show interview, the host asks Neale the quintessential question, "What you're saying is that we're all having a conversation with God? All the time?" Neale answers, "Of course, and it comes to us in all sorts of ways. From the most unexpected sources."

Neale sees an example of the gifts that we are capable of giving to each other in the smiling face of Harry the janitor, who is standing in the wings. Regardless of life's station or status, we actually serve as angels to each other's needs and highest aspirations.

At the end of the filming day, Stephen summoned all cast and crew members into the TV station meeting room and closed the door. Had there been a crisis? Few people knew the purpose of this surprise, insistent gathering. Stephen began by reminding them that the remainder of the movie would be shot on a sound stage, and thus the intermittent exterior days of frigid, cold weather were over. It had been a very demanding shooting schedule, he said, and the total company had responded to all of the challenges magnificently. Then he said that he wanted cast and crew to see the first edit of their efforts—a clip of the opening scenes that set the tone and purpose of the entire movie. The largely unnoticed screen at the front of the room then came to life. They heard wonderful music and saw the homeless camp at Emigrant Lake, and then Henry as Neale as the sun rose in a spectacular birth of morning . . . the magnificent birth of their film. The images brought tears to many eyes as the room filled with spontaneous applause.

Neale's Childhood

Mother, played by Catherine Rowe, and son, played by Suriel Hess-Glover, at the grassy meadow table in Neale's dream

If Neale is taunted by his struggle from homeless failure to world-famous author, he is also haunted by his childhood. At key junctures in the movie, Neale has dreams of being seated with his mother at a table on a grassy meadow. In one dream, his mother tells the panic-ridden child something that becomes seared into his very being. As a man influenced by his *Conversations with God*, Neale visits a cemetery and finds his mother's grave. Finally, he is able to say to her, "You were right about me, Mom, but I'm learning."

I hope that this film does not give anyone a false impression about my childhood. I had a wonderful childhood and wonderful parents. My mother cared for her children deeply and committed herself totally to providing us with a good home, loving values, and a real sense

of the fun and joy of life and all things creative. My father also committed himself to his family. He worked hard to make sure we had everything we needed, gave us examples of strength and stick-to-it-iveness, and had a you can do anything-you-set-your-mind-to kind of courage and confidence that has remained with me to this very day. Likewise, I had wonderful siblings. All of my brothers are terrific, each in his own very special way. I was the youngest of the kids, and so I think I got the best of it all . . . the youngest one almost always does.

So while the moment in this film when my mom did a palm reading for me is true, it does not tell the story of my special relationship with my mother—and of the truly wonderful

person that she was. In fact, it was precisely *because* of that special relationship that her words during that palm reading had such a profound impact on me.

Looking back on it, I think that Mom may have made a mistake telling me something like that when I was a boy—but one mistake does not a bad childhood make, and I had a perfectly glorious childhood, for which I am deeply, deeply grateful.

Shakespeare Square: Neale Meets Someone

SHAKESPEARE SQUARE   SHAKESPEARE SQUARE   SHAKESPEARE SQUARE

A startling climax is about to occur.

Shakespeare Square is the central point of the Oregon Shakespeare Festival and its three theatres that includes the classic Elizabethan Stage. On a cold, rainy night in early December 2005, the *CWG* cast and crew occupied the large semi-circular foyer of the Angus Bowmer Theatre and its exterior courtyard areas for the filming of seven scenes, including the climactic encounter of the film.

The meeting between Neale—and someone who must remain anonymous in this book—is a technical tour de force made possible by a motion control camera head that allows movement on three planes. The motion control device allows two separate shots to be perfectly matched in post-production.

This scene really caught me off guard when Stephen first ran the rough cut past me. It stunned me with its filmatic magic and its powerful imagery. I remember Stephen asking me once during those months leading up to the making of the movie, "In the end, what has the *Conversations with God* experience done for you?"

I replied: "It gave me back to myself. It reintegrated me, it made me whole again. I've always said that the mission of the ReCreation Foundation, which I founded, is to give people back to themselves. We want to help people recreate themselves by getting back to wholeness, by returning them to an experience of *who they really are.*"

Now here I was, watching the end of this movie, in which Stephen had captured the essence of my experience perfectly, using a cinematic metaphor. *What a powerful message!*

I was thrilled.

Visual effects supervisor Jeff Bates watches motion control playback on the monitor with Henry and Dayvin Turchiano, Henry's stand-in.

The last take on the *CWG* set was an exterior at Tark's Market on a Friday night. Stephen rallied the crew to gather around the camera for the last shot, and then he and Henry spoke to those assembled. Those in the crowd included Neale himself and James Twyman, who had come to congratulate their friend Stephen on the completion of principal photography.

Henry was surprisingly emotional in thanking his fellow actors and the crew who had supported him through a sometimes difficult leading role. He said that he would reflect on the experience in January and be better at articulating his perspective then. Stephen was more effusive and unabashedly emotional.

Neale then came through the crowd to embrace Stephen, and with great emotion, Stephen thanked Neale for allowing him to tell the *Conversations with God* story. The two men hugged as the crowd around them applauded.

Although a wrap party was scheduled for the following night, farewells were still being

Stephen clowns with sound man Kent Romney prior to the wrap shots.

expressed. Few cast members remained in Ashland, and many members of the crew had to travel on the weekend to get to new shows on Monday. Most people at the wrap party would be working on the post-production and staying on the job for weeks or months more, but the wrap is always a remembered moment because as a company, many members are preparing to go their separate ways.

I hate goodbyes. I hate them. Why can't people who find each other stay together forever? That's what I want to know. But life is not like that. Life is filled with goodbyes. And I hate it.

I've done a ton of theatre in my life. I mean a ton. I've worked as a sound and light technician, a stage manager, an actor, a director, a musical director and conductor . . . you name it, I've done it. I even did a little musical staging and choreography. And I can tell you that the worst night in any stage production is Closing Night. It's terrible. It's horrible. The group of people who have come together to co-create a magnificent experience will never be together again in just that same way, in that precise grouping, with that identical energy. It's like the end of making love: it's bittersweet. And it's no different on a movie set.

An emotional movie director thanks his cast and crew as principal photography ends.

It was chilly and a bit sprinkly on Wrap Night for this movie. The crew had gathered at a supermarket in Talent, Oregon, jamming the parking lot with trucks and equipment, brightening the night with the huge lights required for shooting movies. Snaking cables were everywhere, laying down tracks for the camera to roll on as it "walked" with Henry, and now the final shot was in the can . . . and then came the words from the director's lips . . . the official announcement that all the filming, every last shot, had been completed: "Ladies and gentlemen, *that's a wrap.*"

A whoop and a cheer went up from the crew . . . but nobody was kidding anybody. There wasn't a dry eye in the space. Everybody, I guess, hates goodbyes. It isn't just people we're saying goodbye to. It's experiences. It's energies. It's territories of the heart.

We know we won't be visiting these territories ever again; maybe look-alike places, but never these exact same territories. And so we weep at goodbyes, some of us inwardly, some of us openly. And then we wrap it up, this golden moment, tying it in a ribbon and holding it forevermore as a golden memory.

Now we can open that package whenever we want and look inside and experience it all over again, and that's the wonder of all the things we've created, and the gift of a good and long life. Yet one day not just a single golden moment, but all the golden moments put together, will be over. We'll wrap them up, tie them in a ribbon, and give them to God. "My life was Your gift to me," we will say, "now here is my gift to You." And God will be pleased with our gift, and smile the smile of a forever love, just as we are pleased with the gifts of our children, no matter how imperfect our children may imagine their gifts to be. We will see them as perfect always, because perfect is exactly, it is precisely, what they are.

And in this way does God see us.

Lisa Schneiderman: Publicist

LISA SCHNEIDERMAN LISA SCHNEIDERMAN LISA SCHNEIDERMAN

Lisa Schneiderman was much more than a publicist for the *CWG* movie. She has also been the personal publicist for both Stephen Simon and Neale Donald Walsch.

Stephen often introduces her as the publicist who launched spiritual cinema as a genre. It was Lisa who booked Stephen on his cross-country speaking tour for *The Force Is with You*. "These two elements were the perfect recipe to help Stephen actualize his dream of bringing forth the voice of his deepest calling. This book and speaking tour set the stage for a movement to be born," Lisa says. The tour branded the term "spiritual cinema" into the film genre vernacular. It was this tour that inspired the birth of spiritual cinema communities throughout the country.

This creative network that was coalescing around Stephen then matured in an ongoing telecourse, an innovative teleconference that allowed people from all over the world to present and discuss spiritual cinema concepts. Out of this intense interest came The Spiritual Cinema Circle. "It was a true honor to help shepherd this concept into the world. Stephen is a tireless advocate in bringing spiritual messages onto the big screen, and he has earned the endearing title of The Godfather of Spiritual Cinema, as many people refer to him. He opened the door for thousands of filmmakers throughout the world to produce and direct conscious filmmaking. The tribe is now in place. It's been amazing to watch it all take form," Lisa adds.

"Lisa was indeed the midwife of spiritual cinema," says Stephen. "She understood my dream from the first time she heard about it. I'll never forget sitting in her office and her asking me to spell out my vision of spiritual cinema for her as she typed at her computer. When we look back now, it's just astonishing to see how many of those dreams have been realized and how many loom so close on the horizon. Lisa's compassion for her clients and her passion for making the world a better place make her the ideal publicist and friend for anyone with a dream that has spiritual roots."

Founder of Schneiderman Public Relations, an entertainment/cause-related boutique agency since 1998, Lisa merged her business in 2003 with legendary Hollywood publicist Lee Solters and his entertainment public relations firm, Solters & Digney, where she became the executive vice president. She now has a growing consulting practice with clients who evoke positive change and raise consciousness in the world through their projects. She acts as both a creative consultant and public relations coach for her clients. Lisa captures the spirit of their message and transforms it to reach a wider, mainstream audience.

*(L to R) DVD producer Ed Keller, moviebook author Monty Joynes, and
Lisa coordinate their interview day in a review of the call sheet.*

Video Store

Andi and Adam Black grew DJS Video from 500 square feet in 1984 to the 20,000 square feet video store of today. It is one of the largest video stores in Oregon, and it is the first movie rental store in North America to devote an entire section to spiritual cinema. Among the five hundred plus titles in the Spiritual Cinema section are the movies mentioned in Stephen Simon's book *The Force Is with You: Mystical Movie Messages That Inspire Our Lives*. The Spiritual Cinema section in this Ashland store debuted in February 2004 with a ribbon-cutting ceremony attended by Stephen Simon, Neale Donald Walsch, and James Twyman.

Recommending spiritual cinema selections has enhanced customer relationships in this independent video store, and the section is now one of its top producing areas. One satisfied customer even sent flowers as a thank you for recognizing spiritual cinema.

Anna Darrah: Director of Acquisitions

ANNA DARRAH   ANNA DARRAH   ANNA DARRAH

Anna Darrah and her precocious daughter Ceryn appear in the Peerless Café scene as extras, but Anna has a key role in spiritual cinema. She is the director of acquisitions for The Spiritual Cinema Circle, which at the time of filming *CWG* had more than 20,000 subscribers.

Anna had been the Events Coordinator of the Santa Fe Film Festival for four years when she convinced Stephen to premiere *Indigo* there. A writer herself, she had previously attended a workshop in association with Stephen's *The Force is with You* book tour. She now thinks of Stephen's cross-country tours as "a gathering of the tribe" of spiritual cinema moviemakers. Anna was ripe to be "gathered."

After participating as an actor in college productions, Anna began a shamanistic spiritual path in her early twenties. "I discovered," she says, "that goals are not things to attain so much as they are experiences to be fulfilled."

In December 2003, Anna originated the acquisitions title that she holds today. Her office is in Santa Fe, where she has a film research assistant. Films are solicited and sent for review, and then Anna screens, rates, and describes them. Only the top one percent is forwarded to Stephen for final selection. He typically approves ninety percent of her recommendations. Then, after selection, Anna sets to acquiring the film rights for distribution. With four films to be acquired every month, Anna keeps busy. "Anna makes my job incredibly easy," says Stephen. "Her taste is impeccable, her empathy with filmmakers is resolute, and she is the single most unflappable person I have ever known. Without Anna . . . no . . . never mind . . . I can't even imagine any sentence that starts 'Without Anna'!"

"The Spiritual Cinema Circle is a new distribution system for independent and grass roots films," Anna says. "If you have a spiritual film, The Spiritual Cinema Circle is the only way to go. We are capable of introducing your film to a huge worldwide audience."

Mark Jennings: Investor and Extra

Mark Jennings came to a crossroads in his life where he learned the difference between achievement and fulfillment by a spiritual process. As an entrepreneur in a private equity company, Mark decided that doing well by doing good was the way that he wanted to do business. A friend introduced him to The Spiritual Cinema Circle in July 2005. After becoming a member and participating in Stephen's telecourse, Mark contacted Stephen to see how he might contribute to the growth of what he considered a synchronistic idea with his own goals. Soon after their dialogue began, Mark was introduced to Gay Hendricks, whom he now considers a mentor.

As the *CWG* film project emerged, Mark assumed a critical financing role. When he read the script and saw the reference to the happy camping family, Mark wanted to be the extra in that scene with his children Kallie and Coleman. He wanted his children to know that their father had a spiritually-oriented nature and that one day, as they saw themselves in the film, they would be drawn to the life lessons that *Conversations with God* contains.

Dr. Richard Kibbey: Investor and Extra

DR. RICHARD KIBBEY DR. RICHARD KIBBEY DR. RICHARD KIBBEY

One of the extras playing a homeless man is Dr. Richard Kibbey, a prominent urologist from Amarillo, Texas. Richard began medical school at age nineteen; and in addition to becoming a community leader, he ran marathons and climbed mountains, including Mt. Rainier. Observers figured from his achievements that Richard was Mr. Perfect, but like so many achievers, he says that he was only seeking approval. After almost dying of pulmonary edema in a South American mountain climb, Richard turned to a spiritual path and began meditating and the study of spiritual disciplines. The path led to a release from social conditioning. He began to express his deepest feelings in poetry.

One synchronistic day, Richard heard an interview with Stephen on Wisdom Radio, and he joined The Spiritual Cinema Circle. When he sent an e-mail to Stephen recommending a book, he was surprised to get a personal response. A dialogue between the two men ensued and then was extended to include Gay Hendricks. Richard felt himself opening emotionally to beauty, nature, and to the people who lived a spiritually conscious lifestyle. When he learned about the pre-production planning for *CWG*, Richard offered to support the project as an investor, and thus he came to see his investment at work on the movie set as an extra.

Melissa and Bob Van Rossum: Investors

MELISSA AND BOB   MELISSA AND BOB   MELISSA AND BOB

*Casting director Kathy Wilson, publicist Lisa Schneiderman,
and investor Melissa Van Rossum gather in the Ashland
Springs Hotel for the open casting call*

Melissa Van Rossum believes that she was an Indigo child, but in the social era of her Atlanta environment the spiritual precocity of children was not encouraged. As an entrepreneurial adult, she began a very successful executive search firm in 1996 that she managed with her husband Bob when they married.

Melissa's interest in Stephen's work came from the importance in her life of his films *Somewhere in Time* and later *What Dreams May Come*. About *Somewhere in Time*, Melissa wrote, "The spirit of that movie spoke directly to me and at a time when I couldn't have needed it more. Looking back, I can see how the metaphysical themes of past lives and reincarnation called to me, but it was something much more than that. Something in that movie spoke to my soul and said, 'There are more of us out here like you, never give up hope.' And so I didn't."

About *What Dreams May Come* she wrote, "I left that movie with the deepest part of my true nature resonating so loudly that I could no longer ignore it. Because of this very special movie, I was beginning to remember who I was and why I was here. You can never go back from that kind of awareness."

While still managing her company, Melissa began writing a book about a method to understand the spiritual reasons of experience. In looking for a creative community to express her work, she participated in one of Stephen's telecourses and then began a friendship with him that led to her interest in playing forward the potential of spiritual cinema as a financial investor.

Melissa had already heard an insistent inner voice telling her, "It's time to go," meaning that she was to leave the management of her business for spiritual work (the book) and for parenthood. Very pregnant with her second son, Melissa made her last trip before delivery to be on hand for the two-day casting call for *CWG* in Ashland. There, she volunteered at the sign-in table and supported the process from start to finish. Her book, now completed, is titled *TruAwareness, the Fast Track to Insight, Healing and Soul Awareness.*

Randi Braham, Location Manager

Alan Mansfield: Investor

ALAN MANSFIELD   ALAN MANSFIELD   ALAN MANSFIELD

Alan Mansfield, a very successful Chicago area industrialist, read *Conversations with God* in 2000 and considered it especially important in his personal life because it validated many of his own thoughts. Alan says that he screamed for joy at the end of the book. "Yes, this is my experience, too." When he learned about the making of a movie based on the book, he made contact with Neale. He says that he was "pushing" himself into a spiritual direction.

Alan met Neale for the first time in person during the third week of filming. They met at the Ashland Springs Hotel for dinner at Lark's, the hotel restaurant. The two men fell into a significant conversation that lasted for three hours.

"I was defined by my business," Alan says. "Now my business does not define me. I am called to a spiritual path. I feel that each piece of my puzzle has come into place."

Alan says that he did not put money into the film as an investor looking for returns. His motivation was the sharing and expansion of a message that had been so transforming in his own life.

Sherril Schlesinger: Post Production Supervisor

SHERRIL SCHLESINGER   SHERRIL SCHLESINGER   SHERRIL SCHLESINGER

It is said in the film business that movies are not made on the set, they are made in the editing suite. It is here that the final assembly is made of all the shots and angles and takes that the director and actors and technicians have created on location. It is here that the pace and impact of the film is created. All the most fabulous footage in the world will yield pitifully little in the hands of a bad editor. Conversely, some of the worst footage ever obtained can be turned into cinematic art by editors who are masters of their craft. When they have wonderful footage *and* a wonderful editor, producers and directors are in heaven.

I've watched Sherril Schlesinger in the editing bay, and all I could say was *Wow! Zounds! That's not possible! You're incredible!* And various incoherent babblings while I shook my head in utter disbelief. Sherril is relentless in her search for the best shot, the best blend, the best connectors, the best sequence and pace and impact. Her sense of what works is impeccable, and her ability to *make* it work is miraculous. Watching her ply the tricks of her trade is enough to make your jaw drop. I've now sat through enough jaw-dropping sessions to know that Sherril Schlesinger is a master at her craft, a genius at her trade.

Sherril began working in films in the mid-1980s in her birthplace of South Africa on *King Solomon's Mines* and its sequel *Allan Quatermain* for Cannon Films. Beginning as a production coordinator, she also has credits as a sound editor, visual effects editor, and post-production supervisor. Sherril has been the assistant editor on more than a dozen feature films and earned the title of Editor on fourteen full-length films, two theme park films for Disney, and another dozen documentaries and short films.

Sherril relocated to Los Angeles in 1990. Her Disney job on *It's Tough to Be a Bug* involved editing 70 mm 3-D animation in conjunction with Pixar. In recent years, she has focused her skills on socially conscious and spiritually oriented films. In documentary form, she has creatively looked at yogis in India and crop circles in England. As a certified energy healer, Sherril sees that her mission is healing through communication. With her passion for storytelling, the making of films that can transform and inspire is the perfect synthesis of what she values most.

In Los Angeles, Sherril heard about Stephen Simon at a time when she was considering leaving film work following two years of training in energy healing. When she went to Stephen's website, however, she found that his sentiments about making movies that matter were totally in alignment with her own hopes and aspirations for the medium. In response, Sherril sent Stephen a very non-Hollywood e-mail introduction that contained an outpouring of her views on the potential of spiritual cinema. She got a personal reply in three days, and six months later Sherril got the editing job on *Indigo* during a conference call with Stephen, Neale, and James Twyman.

Sherril had read *Conversations with God* when it was first published and saw it as a confirmation of her beliefs. Steve, her husband-to-be, had experienced Neale's book as a life-transforming experience. Both believe that *Conversations with God* played a pivotal role in their coming together. The offer for Sherril to edit *CWG* came within the first year of their marriage and work on the film would require her to be absent from their Mar Vista, California home for five months. Another newly married couple might have been unwilling to endure the separation, but this was *CWG* and they willingly embraced it.

"Everything I ever dreamed a filmmaking experience could be is coming true for me on *CWG*," Sherril says. "All my spiritual values are being exercised here. Everyone's place here is important. Everyone feels noticed and appreciated. There are no politics. We are a generous, loving community.

"For instance, my assistant editor Brent Streeper has been an incredible support to me throughout the editing process. Although we had more than our fair share of challenges with faulty drives and numerous other computer quirks, Brent was relentless in figuring out how to keep me moving forward. If it took working through the night—that's what he did. His work ethic is exemplary. He is one of the most hardworking, funny and fun (did I say smart?) assistant editors I could have hoped to work with. I am so grateful to him for being him.

"I've never had a relationship with a director like I have with Stephen. So open, and honest, and yes, emotional. Stephen leads with his heart in everything. He is so focused in gratitude to everyone around him. This is a unique and wonderful experience in a brilliant man. The first screening of the film occurred on my birthday. Amid the tidal wave of details, Stephen produced a huge birthday cake for me and complimented me to tears at the dinner party that followed.

"I have worked harder on *CWG* than on any other film, but after a sixteen-hour day at the editing console, there is no resentment. I only feel the safety of the heart space that is at work in this process. Once, when Stephen and I were debating the cutting of a scene, I said, 'Okay, we'll do it your way. You're the boss.'"

"No," Stephen corrected. "I'm your co-pilot."

"If anyone ever deserved the title of 'unsung hero,' it is Sherril," Stephen says. "Having worked together on *Indigo*, I called Sherril as soon as we knew we were going to actually be shooting the film. As I knew that we were going to be editing here in Ashland, I had some real concerns as to whether Sherril would actually move up here for five months, particularly in light of the fact that she was in the first year of a wonderful marriage. When she agreed to edit the film, I was incredibly relieved (and also eternally grateful to her wonderful husband, Steve.)

"As an editor, her touch is delicate, insightful, and brilliant. Despite some terribly daunting logistical hurdles, she put an entire cut together of the film within ten days after we finished shooting. And, truthfully, there was only one scene in the entire movie where we disagreed on the editing approach. That's one out of 132! By being so in tune with the vision of the movie, Sherril gave us the wonderful luxury of only having to decide WHAT to trim out, not HOW to edit the film. That saved hundreds of hours of work. She just has these incredible instincts and insights about editing material together that make a director's job in the editing room very easy indeed.

"Sherril is endlessly patient, kind, and supportive to the max. She is also as dedicated a person as I have ever encountered. As she also served as both music editor and post-production supervisor, she would think nothing of 18–20 hour days if she felt the film required it. Sherril is really the human prototype/poster person, I believe, for Spiritual Cinema: an incredibly talented, dedicated professional who believes passionately in the spiritual material on which she is working. That's Sherril Schlesinger—the angel/goddess of the editing room."

Jeff Bates: Visual Effects Supervisor

JEFF BATES   JEFF BATES   JEFF BATES

CWG includes some visual effects designed as clever artistic elements to support the storyline. For the car crash, Henry's horror in being broadsided is made visceral by a composite of the green screen shots of a camera car and glass breakaway patterns added to the windshield and rearview mirror.

In the dream sequences of mother and son on a grassy meadow across all four seasons the characters were shot against a green screen, and then matte painters created the seasonal changes by referencing a four-season stock photographic portfolio. The trick for Jeff in the digital process of assembling the elements was to get the feel of the three-dimensional environment right on the screen.

Another tricky visual effect involved the unemployment office scene. Neale is pictured entering the building by going up a staircase, but the set itself was built in the basement of the building with a bothersome window that reeked "basement" and not "second floor." In every frame that showed the basement window, a visual effect was required to make the view appear from a second floor, and in every camera angle change, the altered perspective required a new effort. Small detail? Not if you care about cinematic art.

Visual effects supervisors like to be on set as much as possible to confer with the director and cinematographer. During the climactic scenes of the film, when the crucial last shots required special motion control equipment, Jeff was a key player in planning the matching shots that made possible the technical wizardry in the post-production editing suite.

Jeff holds a master's degree in filmmaking and has twenty-five years of experience as a director and editor. His credits include award-winning television commercials for national clients, documentaries, and music videos for prominent American and Canadian recording artists. As a partner in Jackhammer Films, he is at home in the Northwest with his wife and five children.

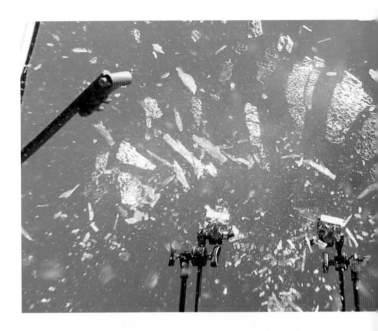
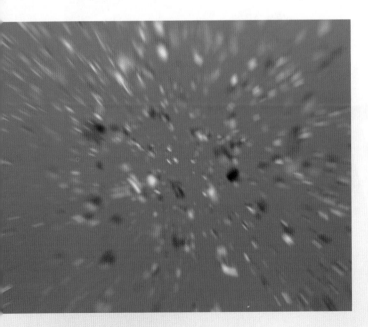

Neale's car crash is a composite of film elements that make for a realistic visual effect on screen.

Emilio Kauderer: Composer

EMILIO KAUDERER EMILIO KAUDERER EMILIO KAUDERER

Emilio Kauderer was born in Argentina, where he trained as a classical pianist. His rigorous academic training in composition and conducting continued on a full merit scholarship at the Tchaikovsky Moscow Conservatory. Emilio's fourteen albums demonstrate a remarkable virtuosity of styles; but whether the music is a movie soundtrack or a collection of romantic Latin songs, his gift for memorable melodies is apparent. He can make his themes soar or allow them to become intimately tender.

On the soundtrack side of filmmaking, Emilio has composed music for more than forty feature films, shorts, and television series since 1980. On the classical side, he has composed chamber music suites, piano concertos, wind quintets, a clarinet suite, and a symphony that has been performed by both the National Symphony of Argentina and the Honduras National Symphony.

In 2001, Emilio was honored by the Sundance Institute with a fellowship to its Composer's Lab, and then he was selected to compose the music for the main exhibit at New York's Museum of Tolerance. Emilio was awarded a Latin Grammy 2003 for *Bajo Fondo Tango Club* produced by Oscar winner Gustavo Santaolalla. Emilio was also nominated for an Emmy for best score, in collaboration with Stewart Copeland, for the Showtime series *Dead Like Me*. Stephen Simon employed Emilio's compositions for *Quantum Project* and *Indigo* before asking him to compose the soundtrack for *CWG*.

Emilio has an underlined second edition copy of *Conversations with God, Book One* from 1996 and he and fellow musicians even met during that period for workbook sessions. When Emilio got the *CWG* film script and began his thematic compositions, he returned to the book and marveled at his underlinings as a measure of what it had meant to him. He was so inspired that he developed the major musical themes of the film from the script months before he actually saw a screening.

The major themes composed for *CWG* are lush, compelling, and even driven in part to reflect Neale's struggle. There are also layers of orchestration within the themes that allow for musical development throughout the movie.

Stephen says of Emilio: "*CWG* is our third film together and by far the most challenging. When I sent Emilio the script, I told him right up front that we needed a signature score for the film. A score that helps define forever what the film is. I had that kind of score only one other time in my career—*Somewhere in Time*. It was very clear to me that *CWG* would require that same kind of emotional, haunting, mystical music that define films like *Somewhere in Time*. Emilio started writing music the minute he read the script, so by the time we had finished the film, he already had several themes ready for us to hear. And hear we did! I believe that Emilio has written one of the most memorable scores I have ever heard. I know that's a grand statement but, if anything, I may be understating the point. He has written a score which, I believe goes right into our hearts and remains there—resonating the emotions of the film. I cannot imagine the film without Emilio's music and, fortunately, all of us will have that music to savor forever."

David Van Slyke: Supervising Sound Designer

DAVID VAN SLYKE   DAVID VAN SLYKE   DAVID VAN SLYKE

A film that has been shot, edited, and scored does not come to life until the sound designer creatively mixes all the elements of spoken dialogue, ambient sounds, music, and sound effects into a convincing reality. The sound components may involve ADR technology to replace dialogue or the Foleying of subtle sounds that the production microphones missed. In working with Emilio Kauderer's score for *CWG*, David was impressed by its engaging, soothing, and contemplative aspects.

On *CWG*, there was a unique challenge to render the voice of God. In the first recorded reading of *Conversations with God, Book One*, the solution was to have the voice change genders, with Ed Asner and Ellen Burstyn alternating in their responses to Neale. In the movie, the voice becomes much more personal in nature. If, as Neale believes, God talks intimately to everyone, then the voice is that of the Self.

David Van Slyke has been nominated for five Emmy awards in sound, and he took home an Emmy for one of his episodes of *CSI*. In 2006, he was nominated twice for the Golden Reel—the Sound Editor's guild award—for episodes of *CSI*, including a two-hour TV program. His sound department filmography includes more than thirty major credits dating from 1990.

David met editor Sherril at one of Stephen's Spiritual Cinema programs at the Agape Spiritual Center in Los Angeles. From the platform, Stephen indicated that he and Sherril were looking for a sound designer for *Indigo*. Many people afterward sought Sherril's attention, but quietly David only asked her to take his card. With David's impressive credits and his purposeful compatibility, one interview sealed the association. The Agape Spiritual Center connection is shared by Sherril, David, and also by *CWG* screenwriter Eric DelaBarre.

"David's amazing 'ear' and sense of place and time in sound design is one of the many reasons that he is another essential member of the core team that worked together on *Indigo* and now again on *CWG*," says Stephen. "Having worked together before, David, Joao, Sherril, Emilio, Renee, and I have created a wonderful filmic shorthand with each other. Joao's images, Sherril's editing, Emilio's music, Renee's designs, and David's sound editing create together much of the tapestry upon which the film plays out."

Ben Lipsey: Still Photographer

Ben Lipsey calls himself a "multimedia production artist." He says, "I'll do anything that allows me to be creative and part of a production that I can be proud of." A graduate of Hampshire College and the son of a professional photographer, Ben worked in Boston and New York as a video editor before being lured to the Portland independent film scene, where he is a freelance photographer for films, concerts, and advertising. Ben had worked on ten feature films produced in Oregon before production coordinator Dawnn Pavlonnis recommended him for *CWG*.

Ben got the photography job based on his website portfolio, but he was also expected to drive a camera truck and to be a set production assistant. The demands of movie-book photography, however, soon had Monty, the book's author, lobbying for Ben's release from all other duties: "It seemed that whenever I directed Ben towards a shot on set, he had already taken it. I soon learned, after the first week's edit, to celebrate Ben, not direct him."

During filming, Ben's father Steve came from Boston and was invited on set with his camera. Most of his pictures, however, turned out to be his children at work—Ben with his camera, and daughter Rachel, the key at Craft Service, and also known as Snack Girl, tending to cast and crew from her snacks and beverages bus.

The challenge of movie still photography is that the set is never under the photographer's control. Rehearsals are sometimes "closed," and some interior sets are too small to enter without interference. Aside from technical skill and a talented eye, movie photography requires patience and a winning personality that invites cooperation when the camera's subjects are often under stress. Ben Lipsey has got all those attributes covered.

Ed Keller: Behind the Scenes DVD

Ed works with CWG DVD producer Jackson Rowe

Ed Keller is the interviewer, cameraman, and editor who produced the *CWG* documentary movie and monthly *Behind the Seen* video diaries for The Spiritual Cinema Circle. He is the chief executive of Edify Productions, an audio-visual company supporting projects that enhance personal spiritual growth. Ed has produced video programs for Neale Donald Walsch, James Twyman, and Gary Zukav in addition to Stephen Simon's *Indigo*, and now *CWG*.

Ed once interviewed for a job with a radio station program director named Bob White. He didn't get the job, but he and Bob White liked each other. Ed's wife had a metaphysical teacher named Neale Donald Walsch that she wanted Ed to meet. On the way to the appointment, a car passed. Ed said, "There goes Bob White."

"No," his wife said firmly. "That's Neale Walsch." The ensuing argument was settled when they arrived at Neale's office. Bob White was Neale's professional radio name and had been for his entire radio career. He was never Neale Donald Walsch on the radio.

While Neale was struggling to get *Conversations with God* published, the Kellers—with a young daughter and baby son—shared the resources of a house and an office with him. Ed personally made the copies of the *Conversations with God* manuscript that was first sent to publishers.

As someone trained for technical theatre (sound and lights), Ed was a natural videographer. As Neale's recognition grew, Ed became the technical manager for *Conversations with God* retreats, and he created the first audio-visual products that expanded Neale's work. Ed also served as the first director of the *Conversations with God* Foundation and later as its audio-visual products director before founding his own production company.

Monty Joynes: The Making of the Movie Book Author

Monty, with his wife Pat, his movie-book assistant, on wrap night

I met Neale Donald Walsch in 1995 at publisher Bob Friedman's home during the Virginia Festival of the Book. Both Neale and I were guests there for the three-day event. Although *Conversations with God, Book One* was published, it was the first time that Bob and his sons Jonathan and Matthew had met Neale in person. Neale and I enjoyed each other, and for the next three years, we met again at Bob's house for an annual reunion of Hampton Roads Publishing Company authors. My wife Pat and I read Neale's *Conversations with God* books as they were published and recommended them to family and friends. Meanwhile, Bob was publishing the four novels in my Booker Series—*Naked into the Night* (1997), *Lost in Las Vegas* (1998), *Save the Good Seed* (1999), and *Dead Water Rites* (2000)—and I was writing other novels and non-fiction books.

Monty reviews a call sheet with actor Bruce Page.

In March 2004 Bob Friedman asked me to go on the set of James Redfield's *The Celestine Prophecy* to develop a making-of-the-movie book. A yearlong effort resulted in the publication of *The Celestine Prophecy: The Making of the Movie* in October 2005. I was not new to movie sets, but it had been a long time since I had written and directed short films shot in Sweden and Austria. New relationships in the film industry, however, encouraged me to write four screenplays before traveling to Ashland, Oregon from Boone, North Carolina to do a second movie book for Hampton Roads Publishing Company.

Basically, my job when writing movie books is to create a narrative that not only documents the movie making experience but also captures, in a literary way, the spiritual essence of the story. By observing on the set and interviewing both cast and crew, I look for a concept of what the book will become. Since filming itself does not follow the storyline, but is dictated by location, I must somehow invent a way to evoke the sense of the film in a non-linear way. This craft challenge of how the book can be organized front to back takes months to digest and assemble from fragments written on set. Then this manuscript is matched with production still photos, production design art, and frames from the movie itself. As editor of all

Monty talks to Henry Czerny as they set up the movie-book's cover shot.

these images, I examine about 5,000 images to deliver something around 160 that appear in the book.

From the day that I accepted the *CWG* assignment, I wondered how Neale himself might be included in a book that expanded the vision of a movie about his own life. Neale and I arranged to discuss his participation in the movie book at his home in Ashland soon after I arrived during the rehearsal week prior to the start of principal filming. Neale was not only as cordial and friendly as I remembered, but he also had a wonderful idea about our collaboration that was easy for me to endorse. After my narrative was completed, Neale offered to write a running commentary that would add his personal insights to the major body of the work. I saw this enhancement as something unprecedented in moviemaking literature, and thus a happy agreement was made.

Although I had been introduced to Stephen Simon briefly in Virginia Beach by Bob Friedman in the summer of 2005, I was not prepared for his generous inclusion of me on his movie set. As both producer and director, Stephen had every excuse to be distant and preoccupied. I witnessed the demands placed upon him, and there was no way that he was getting much more than three to four hours of sleep a day during the production. And yet, despite the pace, whenever you got Stephen's attention you got all of him. He is a unique soul for whom you want to do your best work.

Thank you, Neale and Stephen, for including me in the wonderful process of making *Conversations with God* the movie.

An Afterword from Neale

AFTERWORD   AFTERWORD   AFTERWORD

This book hopes to send the same message as the movie of *Conversations with God* itself: That God is talking to all of us, all of the time. That we are never alone. That we are all one. And that no matter what our circumstance or situation, we can start over at any time and create a new reality.

I am grateful to my friend Monty Joynes for his wonderfully creative work in producing this book, and to my longtime cohort Bob Friedman for publishing it. My deep appreciation goes to Gay Hendricks and The Spiritual Cinema Circle and to Stephen Simon for putting *Conversations with God* on film and making its message available to a wider audience. And my highest thanks go to God, the best friend I ever had, for allowing me to be used in a small way in the sending of God's biggest truth to the entire world.

I only wish our world's spiritual leaders would join with us in the sharing of this truth. The greatest day in the history of the world will be the day that all the world's spiritual leaders stand up together and make a joint announcement to all the people of the world:

WE HEREBY DECLARE THAT THERE IS NO MAJOR DIFFERENCE BETWEEN US OR BETWEEN OUR MESSAGES. AT ITS BOTTOM LINE, YOU CANNOT DISTINGUISH ONE FROM THE OTHER BECAUSE THIS MESSAGE IS FROM GOD AND THERE IS ONLY ONE GOD AND THEREFORE THERE IS ONLY ONE MESSAGE. THAT ONE MESSAGE IS SIMPLY THIS: LOVE ONE ANOTHER.

IF THERE IS ONLY ONE GOD, WHY ARE THERE DIFFERENT RELIGIONS? FOR THE SAME REASON THAT THERE ARE DIFFERENT CULTURES, DIFFERENT LANGUAGES, DIFFERENT COUNTRIES AND LIFESTYLES, AND DIFFERENT COLORS AND SIZES AND SHAPES OF EVERYTHING: WE ARE EACH AN INDIVIDUAL EXPRESSION OF THE DIVINE, AND OUR INDIVIDUAL WAY OF EXPRESSING THE DIVINE WAS INTENDED TO BE OUR GLORY, NOT OUR DOWNFALL. WE BEG YOU, THE PEOPLE OF THE WORLD, TO ALLOW IT TO BE OUR GLORY AGAIN.

Additional Still Photo Credits

PHOTO CREDITS   PHOTO CREDITS   PHOTO CREDITS

All photographs are by Ben Lipsey except those noted below.

Movie frames by cinematographer Joao Fernandes.

Sequence in Book	Description and by-line
25	Gay Hendricks by David Baker
66	Muriel Stockdale by Trix Rosen
135	Restored picnic grounds by Patricia Joynes
154	Downtown Ashland by Patricia Joynes
194	Emotional movie director by Patricia Joynes
202	Kathy, Lisa, Melissa by Dean & Shianna Walker
210	Emilio Kauderer by Martin Bonetto
212	David Van Slyke by Jeremy Balko
214, 215	Ben Lipsey by Steve Lipsey

Hampton Roads Publishing Company
publishes books on a variety of subjects,
including metaphysics, spirituality,
health, visionary fiction, and other related topics.

For a copy of our latest trade catalog,
call toll-free, 800-766-8009,
or send your name and address to:

Hampton Roads Publishing Company, Inc.
1125 Stoney Ridge Road
Charlottesville, VA 22902
E-mail: hrpc@hrpub.com
Internet: www.hrpub.com

Conversations with God

THE MAKING OF THE MOVIE

Monty Joynes

with

Neale Donald Walsch

HAMPTON ROADS
PUBLISHING COMPANY, INC.

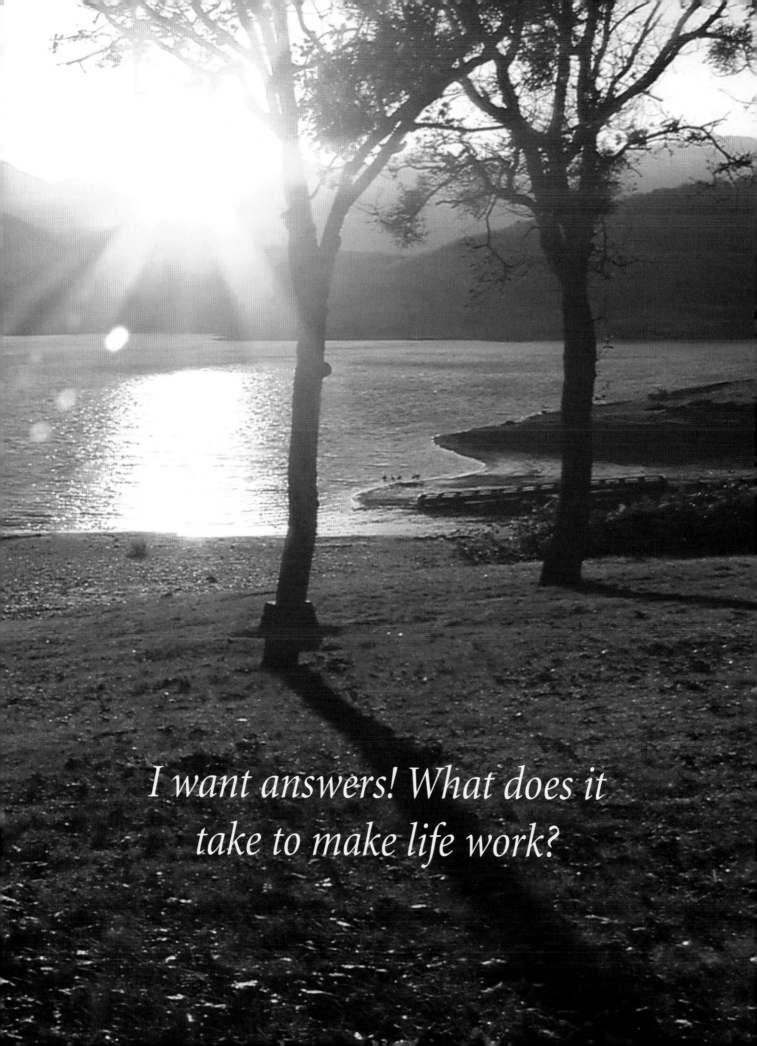

I want answers! What does it take to make life work?

Cover and book design by Frame25 Productions
Cover photo by Ben Lipsey

Hampton Roads Publishing Company, Inc.
1125 Stoney Ridge Road
Charlottesville, VA 22902

434-296-2772
fax: 434-296-5096
e-mail: hrpc@hrpub.com
www.hrpub.com

If you are unable to order this book from your local
bookseller, you may order directly from the publisher.
Call 1-800-766-8009, toll-free.

Library of Congress Cataloging-in-Publication Data

Joynes, St. Leger.
   Conversations with God : the making of the movie / Monty Joynes, with Neale Donald
Walsch.
      p. cm.
   Summary: "Providing an in-depth look at the film adaptation that retraces the rise of Neale
Donald Walsch from homeless man to bestselling author, this making of the movie book
features commentary from Walsch throughout, as well as a selection of photographs from
set locations in southern Oregon"--Provided by publisher.
   ISBN 1-57174-499-1 (8 x 10 tc : alk. paper)
   1. Conversations with God (Motion picture) 2. Walsch, Neale Donald. I. Walsch, Neale
Donald. II. Title.
   PN1997.2.C668J69 2006
   791.43'72--dc22
                                                        2006014776

ISBN 1-57174-499-1
10 9 8 7 6 5 4 3 2 1
Printed on acid-free paper in China

Contents

CONTENTS   CONTENTS   CONTENTS

From Book to Movie

FROM BOOK TO MOVIE   FROM BOOK TO MOVIE   FROM BOOK TO MOVIE

In the spring of 1992, at almost the exact same time that Neale Donald Walsch began receiving answers that would later become his book, a junior at James Madison University in Virginia—Jonathan Friedman—came up with a title for a story or film. The title obsessed him until he wrote a short story with that title a year later in his fiction writing class. The story title was *Conversations with God*.

Flash forward to October 1994. Jonathan Friedman is having lunch with his father, a publisher, in his dad's office. Jonathan is an hourly wage employee mostly involved with data processing. He does not read manuscripts nor does he care to; he has his own creative ambitions. A book manuscript, one being reconsidered, is face down on his father's desk. The manuscript is being reviewed a second time after being previously rejected because the author had insisted that he would accept a rejection only if the publisher first read any ten pages again.

For some reason Jonathan picks up the manuscript, turns it over, and reads the title. The coincidence of the title being the same as one of his own prompts Jonathan to read random pages. He is amazed to find that this author has asked some of the same questions that his character posed to God in his college short story. With Dad's permission, Jonathan takes the manuscript of Neale Donald Walsch's *Conversations with God* home that evening, and by morning he has read it through. Jonathan shares the manuscript with his brother Matthew, and the twenty-something brothers sum up the power of the book for themselves by saying, "We have never seen words used to express with such spectacular clarity the emotional and spiritual convictions we all share but have such difficulty communicating."

The next day, Jonathan hands the *Conversations with God* manuscript back to his father, Robert Friedman, president of Hampton Roads Publishing Company, and says, "You have to publish this book! It's going to sell millions!" His father has already fallen in love with the book, but when he hears that comment he replies, "Yeah, right, kid!" Jonathan is soon on the phone to Neale, telling him about the title coincidence, his confidence in the book's success, and an image he'd once conceived for a poem that he had written and that now seems to him

Conversations with God

• an uncommon dialogue •

book 1

Neale Donald Walsch

the perfect image for the book's cover. Neale approved of Jonathan's intuition and the project raced forward. Jonathan was adamant about every design feature of the book, and he was able to convey his poetic image to artist Louis Jones, whose cover art has appeared on all editions of the book. Remarkably, *Conversations with God* hit bookstores only four months after being accepted by Bob Friedman.

During 1995, after Hampton Roads released *Conversations with God*, Jonathan, by then Neale's friend and confidant, devoted himself to the book's promotion and distribution. His tireless efforts played a major role in pushing the book to its first 100,000 sales. After that, success was guaranteed. Putnam took *Conversations with God* worldwide and made it a bestseller, confirming Jonathan's original evaluation of the book.

In his introduction to the first *Conversations with God* book, Neale says, "The book was not written *by* me, it *happened* to me. We are all led to the truth for which we are ready." When the book first appeared, religious critics called Neale a blasphemer, a fraud, and a hypocrite for not having lived the life of a holy man. Neale also posed these hard questions to himself. Was the book the product of "a frustrated spiritual imagination or simply the self-justification of a man seeking vindication from a life misled?" The reaction of people who read and responded to the book convinced Neale that the power of the document far exceeded his own ability to create it.

The book, in fact, became Neale's teacher—a personal teacher that spoke to him in his own vernacular, offering him explanations that were both theological and spiritual. This teacher also gave practical answers to questions about relationship, sex, power, money, and

health. From Neale's point of view, God had not stopped communicating two thousand years ago. God is continually communicating about every aspect of human life to anyone who will listen—not just to holy men, medicine women, shamen, and mystics. "God talks directly to everyone," Neale said. "Saint and sinner, the good, the bad, and the ugly." For many, many people around the world, this idea alone was transforming.

Neale completed *Conversations with God, Book One* in February 1993 and wrote the introduction during Christmas of 1994. When *Conversations with God* became a worldwide bestseller ideas and offers to turn it into a movie abounded. However, a man writing on yellow legal pads was not visually interesting and, more troublesome, who would play God? The key to making a movie around Neale's revelations required focusing on Neale's personal struggle as a psychologically destitute and homeless man. This true-to-life and extremely personal event did provide a storyline that could be dramatized. But how were the Homeless Neale and the Book Neale to co-exist in the same film, and how could the wisdom of *Conversations with God* be conveyed to the movie audience without any aspect of preachiness?

Neale's Commentary

I can't even begin to explain how surreal it is to have someone tell you they are going to make a movie of your life. It is very, very strange and very, very scary on a lot of levels. It is also a bit disconcerting to see what this does to one's ego. Mine, anyway.

I have to admit that I was filled with egocentric thoughts when the idea behind *Conversations with God* the movie (*CWG*) was first proposed to me in a serious way. This welling up of ego was followed by shame and guilt as I re-embraced a previously well understood truth that this story is not about me at all, but rather about every human being, and that by thinking of it in strictly personal terms I, myself, was missing the entire message of the book! Then came fear. I was afraid that movie-makers would *miss the same message!*

Let me back up here and say that from shortly after the publication of *Conversations with God* and the surprising early acceptance and embracing of this astonishing material in countries around the globe I knew that the book's message was not meant for me alone, but was intended for the entire world. From the moment I reached that clarity, I wanted *Conversations with God* to be made into a movie. I knew of the power of motion pictures to send messages through the use of images and the feelings they evoke. They say that a picture is worth a thousand words—and they're right.

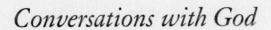

Conversations with God

• an uncommon dialogue •

book 2

Neale Donald Walsch

When I saw how fast my ego took over shortly after I knew that a movie was really going to be made, however, I saw my own weakness. And, I began to worry that the producers would fall into their own weakness as well—a need to "Hollywoodize" the story to make it a "good sell," regardless of whether the film wound up distorting the book's message, or perhaps even losing it entirely.

So, a lot of stuff was coming up for me around this whole experience. It was a real rollercoaster ride. Things settled down, I'm happy to say, after my first substantive conversations with Stephen Simon, the film's eventual producer/director, in November 2004. Stephen had wanted to make *CWG* for a number of years, but I'd told him not to come to me with any kind of chatter about a film until he knew he had the funding to make one. (I hate to get all excited over nothing.) It was at that early November meeting when Stephen told me that sufficient funding had finally been found for the project, so I knew that at last this was serious, that it was going to happen. I told Stephen to send me a letter with his proposal, which he did a few days later and which I then forwarded to my literary agent in New York. A month later *we* had a deal. *Now* I had something to get *excited about.*

Stephen and I met again, and he outlined his ideas for the project and, most importantly, he gave me his personal assurance that I would be a full partner in the undertaking who could provide meaningful consultation at every step along the way.

He kept his word, as I knew he would.

I'd known Stephen for several years, having met him just prior to the release of a film that he'd co-produced, *What Dreams May Come.* I experienced Stephen to be a person of

Neale and Stephen, a happy collaboration

impeccable personal integrity: a man who means what he says, says what he means, and does what he agrees to do.

Stephen told me he wanted to make the movie because he had a real desire to send the message of *Conversations with God* to a wider audience. It was a message in which he fervently believed, by which his life had been deeply touched, and through which he'd come to remembrances that richly expanded his experience of self. He wanted the whole world to hear its truth.

I wanted that, too. And so from the beginning we were both on the same page. When I found out in that November 2004 meeting that funding for the movie was coming from The Spiritual Cinema Circle, I was elated! That meant that Gay and Kate Hendricks were going to be part of the game, and that closed the deal for me. As had Stephen, I'd known Gay and Katie for some time, and I could think of no other people with whom I would rather partner

Conversations with God

• an uncommon dialogue •

book 3

Neale Donald Walsch

in moving the message of *Conversations with God* further into the world.

Stephen made it clear at the outset that the movie would have to be centered on certain events in my life. A film has to tell a *story*, after all; it cannot be just the recounting of a conversation. But Stephen also was emphatic in his determination that this not turn into a "bio pic." He settled early on an organizing theme for the screenplay: It happened to him and it can happen to you. He wanted his audience to understand that what was going on with Movie Neale was going on with everyone. Stephen was also insistent that the device of storytelling be used to send the *messages* of *Conversations with God* through dialogue and on-screen action. He was determined that the messages not be lost but, quite to the contrary, pop up everywhere. Thus began the process of getting *Conversations with God* from book to movie.

The serious work got underway in January 2005. Stephen and I had decided on Eric DelaBarre as our screenwriter. I first met Eric in my home in December 2004 when he came to interview for the writing job. I knew after talking with Eric for just a few minutes that he was the person I wanted to write the screenplay. I could only hope that Stephen felt the same way. As in almost every decision that was made on this project, Stephen and I did agree. Often, we would say the exact same words at the exact same time in discussions about the movie—so close was our agreement, so much were we in harmony. It's a real gift to the whole project when the people behind it think so much alike.

Eric, too, fell into this harmony. His reasons for wanting to work on the film were identi-

cal to Stephen's and mine. He, too, had been deeply touched by the *Conversations with God* material and he, too, only wanted to present its message to a wider audience. This stood in sharp contrast to some of the other L.A. screenwriters who'd been approached or who approached us, most of whom saw the project as interesting but, in the end, not much more than another employment opportunity. To this harmonious triumvirate Stephen invited Viki King, a well known and widely respected Hollywood script consultant with a deep spiritual awareness and a true desire to share larger messages through cinematic art.

So it was that in January 2005 the four of us sat down together in my living room in Ashland, Oregon and began working in earnest on the project. Also in the room were Jackson Rowe, a soft spoken and endlessly helpful young man who was acting as Stephen's closest personal assistant at this point on the project, and Joao Fernandes, whom Stephen had asked to serve as direc-

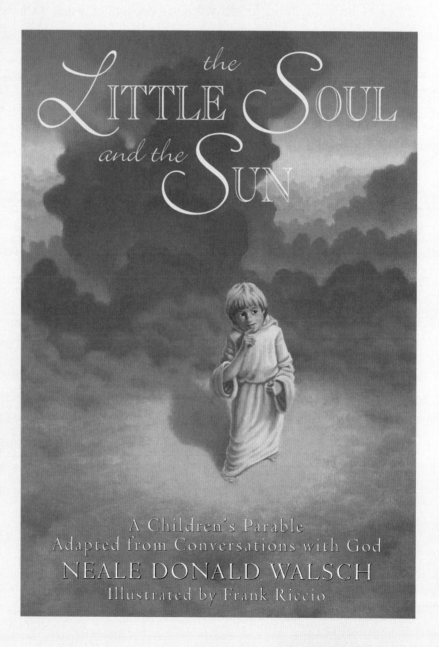

tor of photography (and about whom I will have more to say later).

This was when things became surreal again. Try to picture this—and try to put yourself *into* this picture. A Hollywood producer/director, screenwriter, script consultant, and master cinematographer are sitting in your living room discussing how to film the story of your life. How much should be told? How much is relevant to the purpose of the movie? How can we transfer these events to film?

Again, we all agreed at the outset that this was not really a story of my life, but a film that would *use* certain elements and events *from* my life to tell a *larger* story.

the LITTLE SOUL and the SUN

A Children's Parable
Adapted from Conversations with God
NEALE DONALD WALSCH
Illustrated by Frank Riccio

Still, it was surreal because the first thing we did was get those elements down on paper. Everyone was asking me, "What happened? Tell us exactly what happened. And *then* what happened? And *then,* and *then*?" Eric was taking notes like crazy on his laptop, clicking away at the keyboard with my every utterance. My God, I kept thinking, I hope I'm remembering all this right. This man is carving this in *stone.*

I began to get nervous, especially when they all started asking me for details about details. I was asked questions I never expected to be asked—especially by Viki, who specializes in getting to the story behind the story (what she calls "the *real* story"), and who plumbs the deepest inner nuances that form the *backdrop* against which contemporary events occur.

I remember at one point feeling as though I was being analyzed. Yet it was precisely this deep probing that elicited my account of a childhood event involving my mother that I never thought had anything to do with my present-day experience. Viki assured me it did, and everyone else in the room agreed that it was and is an integral part of the whole *Conversations with God* experience. That childhood event—something I've thought about many times but not something that I imagined had a place in the movie—made its way into the finished film . . . as a pivotal element. So much for my knowledge of how to create a script! This is where Viki and Eric shone however, so I knew the project was in good hands.

One thing I hadn't counted on in the early scripting process was that in going over the specific events of my life, I would wind up reliving them. Casually remembering something is one thing, but being asked to describe a circumstance or event in every detail is quite another. It throws the mind back into not just a remembrance, but a re-experiencing. I found myself emotionally all over the place during this process. Never more so was this the case than when all six of us piled into a couple of cars and went out to the campsite, which is still there, where I lived for so long.

Now here I was walking in the same places, taking some of the exact same *steps* that I had taken as a homeless person, when I scoured the dumpsters for treasures and trudged along in the mud on rainy nights looking for soda and beer cans that I could pick up and take to the store for the five cent return deposit. At one point during this tour I was overwhelmed by the memories and began to choke up. Stephen and the others gently comforted me.

The journey from book page to movie frame had only just begun of course and I won't go on and tell the whole story here because that's what this book is about and I don't want to preempt it! I do want to speak to one thing however, and the beginning of this book is just the place to do it.

From those very first discussions about the making of *Conversations with God* into a movie in the days before Thanksgiving 2004 to the moment that actual shooting began almost exactly a year later, I made it very clear to Stephen and everyone else involved in the

creative process that the film could not and would not go into any aspects of my private life having to do with wives and children. I have been married multiple times, and I have nine offspring. I told Stephen that I had already done enough damage to the people closest to me in my life, and I was not going to now subject them to the additional encumbrance of the glare of public portrayal and scrutiny. So it was that at the first scripting conference in January 2005 the ground rule was laid down: "None of Neale's wives and none of his children will be portrayed in this film."

It was agreed that, apart and aside from the personal privacy issue, if we got into even a little *bit* of that personal family stuff in the movie, it would open up many subplot lines, any one of which could be an entire story in itself. On the other hand, to minimize the impact of these persons on the story by including them in the film but skimming over their roles in a fast once-over would be to do them each a greater injustice than simply crafting a script that did not touch on their roles at all. That was the decision that we made.

The movie was not to be an event-by-event, person-by-person story of my life, but the story of how the message of *Conversations with God* came through and of the circumstances leading up to that. Thus, the film was to be tightly focused, not a sweeping saga. And mostly it would be a *dramatization*—with all the creative license that word implies. For the focus of the project was not to be my personal life story, it was to be the *Conversations with God* message.

Our challenge in the scripting conference was to decide *which* events and people and moments from my life to capture, portray, and dramatize. The decision was made to "write around" the people closest to me—and, for that matter, other individuals in my story as well—in order to protect their privacy, as well as to

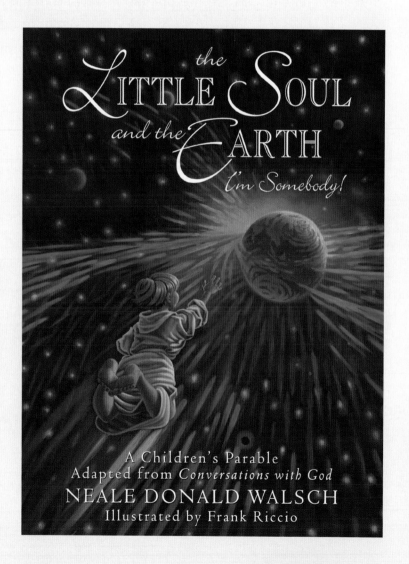

keep the movie from rivaling *Gone with the Wind.* This presented some scripting challenges, as might be imagined. Some of the more distant "characters" in my life story were to become composite characters in the movie. Other characters were "invented" in the film version to represent a dramatized portrayal of an actual person.

One example of this is the character of Oscar, who appears in the movie as the manager of the campground where I lived with other homeless people. There was a manager at this park, but he had none of the characteristics of Oscar. Stephen chose to cast the role of Oscar as he did because of the unique flavor that actor Jerry McGill brought to the part, not because of how closely Jerry resembled the actual manager of the actual park in the actual experience. On the other hand, the man who played the part of the original publisher of *Conversations with God,* an actor named Joe Ivy, looked and acted so much like his real-life counterpart that it was eerie!

To help our audience understand why the film contained no mention or showing of the wonderful women who shared my life during the time many of these events were happening and the children in my life, we put into its very first dialogue scene an exchange (very similar to one that actually took place at one of my on-the-road lectures) in which I explained to a questioner that I was not going to get into matters involving the people who have been closest to me.

Again, all of us on the creative team were determined to keep the film's story limited to how the messages came to a human being. The larger focus in constructing the script was ever and always on the message of *Conversations with God,* not the day-in, day-out details—however important in my personal experience—of Neale Donald Walsch's life.

Stephen, Eric, and Viki had all read the *Conversations with God* material, naturally, but they nevertheless kindly asked me for a list of what I thought were the most important messages of the book. All three reviewed my list and pared it down, and then Eric wove as many of the remaining words into the dialogue as he could without making the movie "preachy." Key and pivotal to all of this was, of course, the work of Stephen Simon, who, as producer/director, was overseeing every detail of the film's production—and none more so than the creation of the script.